# Signatures

# Enslaved

A Chronicle of Resistance
Book 3 – Hidden in Plain Sight

By
Brian Sankarsingh

*And featuring poems by*
Janet L. Wheat-Kaytor
J. E. Rehel
Loretta Laurie Fisher
Sherman K. Francis

SG Productions

First Edition 2023

All rights reserved.

No part of this publication may be reproduced in any form, or by any means, electronic or mechanical, including photocopying, recording, or any information browsing, storage, or retrieval system without permission in writing from SG Productions except in the case of brief quotations embodied in critical reviews and certain other non-commercial uses permitted by copyright law.

For permission requests, write to:
Sankarsingh Gonsalves Productions
c\o brian@sgproductions.ca

ISBN
Softcover - 978-1-7380419-0-9
Hardcover - 978-1-7380419-7-8


Poetry, Canadian

# Praise for Enslaved, A Chronicle of Resistance

"Enslaved" is a very worthy book series! Especially for educational institutions. I am indeed happy to endorse and promote "the Enslaved series" at A Different Booklist bookstore! – **Itah Sadu, award-winning storyteller and author, managing director of the Blackhurst Cultural Centre and co-owner of A Different Booklist.**

\*\*\*

Overall, the book (Enslaved, A Chronicle of Resistance Lamentation of the Enslaved) with a focus on the beginning period of enslavement is a very good educational tool or resource mainly for young adults and youth. It introduces them to the facts of the Atlantic Slave Trade. Young people might not necessarily want to read a textbook account about African enslavement. Poetry can be more digestible at times, and it is an alternative way to expose them to that history and to important related themes. For example, that there was much resistance on the part of the enslaved; and they did not just passively accept the brutality imposed on them. I also appreciated the poems: "Stripped" and "I am Human" because they made very clear that the only way for the enslavement of Africans to happen on such a monstrous scale was by the belief that Africans were not fully human. It is an important point to make because it introduced a conversation about the immorality of the entire practice. People need to know not only the facts and details of what happened, but why it happened and also why it should never happen again." **Geeta Raghunanan, A Different Booklist**

\*\*\*

First and foremost, I feel privileged to have been asked to review this amazing work by a good friend and colleague. I don't consider myself a literary person nor I consider myself a person engaged with history as such. I like to read, and I attempt to familiarize myself with history with the aim of understanding the present.

I am honored to lead an organization established to address the impact of anti-Black racism on the health and wellbeing of Black communities. Reading the series 'Enslaved, A Chronicle of Resistance', not only re-affirmed for me the importance of the movement that uplifts the voice, the struggle, the strength and the dreams and aspirations of the diverse Black communities which was intensified after the painful deaths of George Floyd, Brianna Taylor, Regis Korchinski-Paquet, Joyce Echaquan and many more; but also reminded me that addressing systemic anti-Black racism is a very long and complex journey because it is hidden in plain sight!

Not all good will gestures by the system players are meant to bring about positive change and wellbeing for Black communities. In one of the poem, John Brown, the captain of the ship, has kept the vessel well ventilated. Plainly this is a noble gesture to keep his 'cargo' healthy. But hidden is the motive of preserving the value of the 'cargo' so there is no financial loss. How are we to receive certain legislations, policies, promises from the ship owners and captains of today? Do they have our true wellbeing in mind or does it continue to be about their own self-preservation? A question that continued to resonate with me as I navigated through the pages of the three volumes. "There is a moral to this story hidden in plain sight – not everyone who is fighting for you, May believe in your human right".

When you read about the establishment of the 'Apprenticeship Laws', you cannot but think about the current state of our child welfare system – "So come and give me your children I will make them apprentice, For you cannot even care for them and that fact hurts my conscience". You read about the 15th Amendment and the provision of voting rights. But you also learn about the introduction of the poll tax that prohibited many Black people from not only voting and having their voices heard but also denied them hope and **choice**.

Enslaved – A Chronicle of Resistance comprises of three volumes – The Lamentation of the Enslaved (set between 1700-1800), Freedom Bells are Ringing (1800-1900) and Hidden in Plain sight (present day). The volumes are connected by a very powerful refrain from the Kingdom of Nri (Nigeria), a kingdom of freedom and haven for marginalized peoples. "I am child of the Kingdom of Nri, We believe ALL men are born to be FREE. This gift is granted by Chukwu to all, That enter into Nri's great hall". We are all born FREE. And plainly we are all free where we live today. However, hidden in plain sight are many shackles, chains, constraints, limitations, barriers, and abuses.

Brain Sankarsingh brings these hidden and ongoing issues to the forefront through amazing poetic literature introduced by thought provoking and context setting introductions. One cannot but enjoy his work. – **Liben Gebremikael, Executive Director TAIBU Community Health Centre**

## Table of Contents

Foreword ................................................................................. i

Dedications ........................................................................... iii

Acknowledgements ................................................................. v

About The Cover ................................................................... vii

About Capitalizations and Language Conventions ............... viii

Introduction .......................................................................... ix

I am Jameila Alford ................................................................ 1

Setting the stage .................................................................... 4

Abolition: Disappeared Promises ........................................... 7

Good news…Slavery's Abolished! ........................................ 10

…No! You're wrong! ............................................................ 11

A dream ............................................................................... 13

Three in One ........................................................................ 14

A book ................................................................................. 16

What will tomorrow bring ................................................... 18

One Bad Apple .................................................................... 21

Jim Crow across the Eras: He Never Really Died ................ 23

How the West was raised ..................................................... 25

215 children ........................................................................ 27

Jameila and Grandma Dot .................................................. 29

Oh Canada – Part One ........................................................ 32

It's not all Black and White ................................................. 33

| | |
|---|---|
| A Strange Inconsistency | 35 |
| Plantation Capitalism: A Bitter Sugar Addiction | 37 |
| Break the cycle | 40 |
| Oh Canada – Part Two | 42 |
| Not alone | 45 |
| Still Tricked: Justice is M.I.A. | 47 |
| The Black in BIPOC | 50 |
| The Indigenous in BIPOC | 52 |
| The People of Colour in BIPOC | 55 |
| Rotten House | 57 |
| Amassing Wealth is not Common Wealth | 60 |
| Oh Canada – Part Three | 64 |
| Sinful Fraternization | 66 |
| Part 1 - Female Black Achievers Take On The World | 68 |
| Part 2 - Female Black Achievers Take On The World | 73 |
| Part 1 – Symbols | 76 |
| Random acts of Racism | 77 |
| Part 2 – Symbols | 81 |
| Hidden in Plain Sight | 83 |
| Systemic Change | 86 |
| Documented Facts | 88 |
| Part I - I wish I were Black | 91 |
| Part II – You have no idea what you're talking about | 93 |

| | |
|---|---|
| Part III – And I'm not sorry to tell you so | 95 |
| Oh Canada – Part Four | 98 |
| Enslaved | 99 |
| The Mirror | 101 |
| Destroyed | 103 |
| I don't mean to be racist, but | 106 |
| I'm not racist, I have Black friends | 108 |
| I'm not racist, I have White friends | 110 |
| I don't understand – A question | 111 |
| Let me explain – The answer | 113 |
| Trump card | 115 |
| The Mad King | 118 |
| 1 - Go back to your own country | 120 |
| 2 - No! You go back first | 121 |
| Oh Canada – Part Five | 122 |
| A Legacy of Hate | 124 |
| Being Brown | 126 |
| A White perspective | 128 |
| Doctor Racist | 129 |
| Judge Racist | 131 |
| Officer Racist | 132 |
| Born a Racist | 134 |
| Micro Aggression | 136 |

| | |
|---|---|
| Shades | 140 |
| Black Lives Matter Too | 142 |
| 1ne Race | 143 |
| Jameila's Reflections | 147 |
| …for my young brother, Tony | 150 |
| Tired | 155 |
| The Reality of our Lives | 157 |
| I don't want to World | 161 |
| Duality | 165 |
| 1 - My Brothers, White | 168 |
| 2 - My Brothers, Black | 172 |
| Colour Blindness | 175 |
| Table of Figures | 179 |
| Biographies and Poems | 180 |
|    Brian Sankarsingh | 180 |
|    Janet L. Wheat-Kaytor | 183 |
|    J. E. Rehel | 184 |
|    Loretta Laurie Fisher | 185 |
|    Sherman K Francis | 187 |
| Index | 189 |

# Foreword

I reiterate, at the outset, that I am extremely impressed with the general work and the power that flows off the page. It brings to mind – by virtue of its stridency, courage and creativity – some of the writings of authors like James Baldwin, Maya Angelou, Lorraine Hansberry, George Jackson (whose 'Prison Letters' I was privileged to read, in my very early teens, very many moons ago).

The inclusion of historical fact, with division into three distinct eras, is ingenious. It accurately mirrors the seminal research done by the Caribbean's foremost economist and developmentalist, the late Lloyd Best and Canadian thinker Kari Levitt viz., the Plantation Economy (Pure Plantation, Plantation Modified & Plantation Further Modified – the latter corresponding to the current era). ENSLAVED focusses precisely on these eras, through a more personalized, dramatic, poetic lens.

The accurate portrayal of pre-slavery Africa and its economic and socio-political structures is another case in point. Detailing the horrors of the Slave Trade and the singularity of its profit maximization motive also enhances the work's historical accuracy. As does treatment of 'the white man's burden" – civilizing savages.

The roles of religion and systemic (institutional) racism in facilitating system perpetration and perpetuation, are also well recognized and presented. Well done!

There is a lot more that can be said about Enslaved, A Chronicle of Resistance, all of it complimentary. It would be great to see it added to the existing corpus of relevant literature, and it certainly has my best wishes.

**James Baisden (*12-04-1957 - 15-03-2023*)**
**Educator, Author, Music Producer and Artist**

# Dedications

I am not a Black person, nor do I identify as a Black person. I am, however, a Person of Colour, and I do identify with the struggle of BIPOC peoples.

This book, therefore, is dedicated to Black people, Indigenous people, and People of Colour everywhere and to their continued resistance of White supremacy – **Brian Sankarsingh**

\*\*\*

I would like to dedicate this book to our readers and everyone dealing with racism. To my family and friends who support me and love me no matter what, Tony, Nick, and Jeff, you have my heart. To my best friend, Shelley. To the rest of my family, Joy, Rebecca, Jessalyn, and Cheryl, and to my incredible boss Alexey, and co-worker Nina, my extended family – **Janet L. Wheat-Kaytor**

\*\*\*

My poetry is dedicated to my African Ancestors. Their voices clearly echo through mine. Our heartfelt connection is rooted in systemic oppression which gives fuel to on-going resistance throughout the ages. I appreciate them for wildly cheering me on with the same love and support as my daughters, Leah, Shawna, Maya, and my grandson, Nathaniel. I also appreciate the encouragement of all my comrades at W.A.C, P.A.C and Spring Socialist Network. Special appreciation for my writer siblings: Brian, Sherman, Janet, and Jason, who forged bravely into wicked storms on this epic journey. Last, but not least, my poetry is dedicated to all humans in the process of finding a true path to freedom – **Loretta Laurie Fisher**

\*\*\*

My contribution to this beautiful work of art is dedicated to my wonderful and supportive wife of twenty years, Lisa. To my children, Isaiah, Jovan, Jedidiah and Jazara and to the readers. Be inspired to be advocates for the disenfranchised – **Sherman K. Francis**

\*\*\*

I dedicate these small lyrical contributions to all people and beings who have sought and who still seek freedom from oppression, tyranny and fear. Furthermore, I would like to dedicate this shared collection of work to all who will read it seeking to come away with more understanding, love and shared desire for change in their hearts. This book is for you. Welcome – **Jason E. Rehel**

# Acknowledgements

Without the support and perseverance of my beloved wife and life partner this book would not be possible. It is her strength and optimism that has fueled my own passion for this writing. She is my muse; encouraging, supporting and inspiring me to pursue this crazy dream.

Researching and writing this book involved was so emotionally draining I am thankful for my friends Hari, Zee and Kris - thank you for being there and giving me your support when it was sorely needed brothers. Special thanks to Roberta Shaffer for her editing services.

The idea for Enslaved, A Chronicle of Resistance was conceived in the Summer of 2020 as I prepared to launch my first book. It began as a seed, and I realised that it would be a severe injustice to tend to it on my own. So started the search for other gardeners. There were several failed attempts and with each so grew my desperation. Then suddenly, in the space of a few weeks this talented group of poets came together.

I am grateful for the diversity of this team. Each of these poets have had to struggle with this work. Some from a BIPOC perspective and others from a White perspective.

We had countless difficult discussions about racism, prejudice and hate. But every one of those discussions ended with a deeper understanding and empathy on both sides.

## About The Cover

The upraised clenched fist is the universal symbol of resistance. In 1968 sprinters Tommie Smith and John Carlos made the upraised clenched fist famous. They did this from the top of an Olympic podium during their medal ceremony.

We hope, dear reader, that as you read these poems, Enslaved stands as a clenched fist in the wake of the resurgence of White supremacy and oppression. We hope that you are challenged by to address systemic racism in all its forms and that your own stories will one day become poems.

## About Capitalizations and Language Conventions

In this book, Enslaved, A Chronicle of Resistance, the poets have agreed to capitalize Black and White when referring to racial groups [i]. In the current climate of hate, demonization and polarization we feel it is better to build bridges. This does not mean we diminish or ignore history, after all it is the path that brought us to this place. We risk much more than division between races if we choose to ignore history, we risk our humanity.

We use Canada English conventions in the book.

# Introduction

Enslaved, A Chronicle of Resistance is the first modern book of its kind.

It is a chronicle of enslavement and resistance told in an exquisite blend of prose and poetic verse. Through the esthetic rhythms and rhymes of poetry, it chronicles the establishment and institutionalization of systemic racism. Each poem tells its own story, but each is also part of a bigger narrative. A story, within a story.

A prelude to each poem sets the context and moves the story along. Some of these preludes describe the historical, cultural, societal, political or economic environment as well.

Enslaved, is not just poetry about the atrocities of African slavery and the horrible price humanity continues to pay for it. Neither is it just a story of racism, bigotry, discrimination or prejudice. It is a story about dominion, power and control. It plunges the depths of depravity humanity can sink to and the things they are willing to do to justify it all. It is also a story of hope, courage and optimism as can only be told through poetry. It powerfully tackles the subjects of racism, Shadeism (the discrimination against an individual based on their skin tone), the use of racist symbols and systemic racism in a time when the world is caught up in debate as to what all of that really means. It shows the birth of systemic racism and challenges readers to address it in whatever colour it rears its head.

As humanity stands on a precipice, looking down into the darkness of its own historical hate and racial prejudice, Enslaved, A Chronicle of Resistance, reminds them of past horrors, before challenging them to step back from the precipice.

The United Nations sees slavery as an umbrella term that is related to forced labour, debt bondage, forced marriage and human trafficking[ii]. In other words, any situation(s) of exploitation that a person cannot refuse or leave because of threats, violence, coercion, deception, and/or abuse of power.

Sadly, for as long as humans have wandered the face of this blue planet, some have hungered to exercise dominion over others. This heartless need to dominate and rule over those perceived to be "lesser" or "sub-human", has corrupted and contaminated humanity throughout history. Our conquered enemies become our slaves for life. We demand servitude as payment for debts, real and imagined. Whole clans and tribes serve only as fodder for would-be landowners and royalty because of perceived status.

From the cave to the pyramid, castle to tenement, the hunger to dominate another's life has beleaguered us. When driven by the need to occupy the top of the food chain, many are all too willing to stand upon the lifeless bodies of their fellow human beings.

One practice, however, stands head and shoulders above it all. It is the one that serves as a lesson in what happens when one race uses all its resources, power, abilities and even the moral authority of its religion to rule over another.

The depraved cruelty of the American enslavement trade has eclipsed all other known examples. However, we must acknowledge that a simple reason we are so keenly aware of the atrocities of the American enslavement of Africans is that it is well documented. We have historically accurate records that describe the brutalities done to the African enslaved people. There are court cases where enslavers were tried for killing the enslaved and more recently, historically accurate non-fiction books – and later movies –

that use enslavement as the backdrop of storytelling. These have all served to help preserve Black history.

These series of books walk a fine line between historical fact, fiction and our present reality. The poets acknowledge that they did not write about every single Black person or Person of Colour who resisted enslavement and their ongoing struggle against systemic racism. There were, and continue to be, so many brave and resilient people who engage in this fight. Without their struggle we would all lose; if they are not mentioned here, that does not diminish their contributions.

The story is divided into three books and one companion reader

> **Book 1 - The Lamentation of the Enslaved** set between the 1700s to the mid-1800, examines the beginning of African enslavement and plunges into the pain and struggle of several enslaved Africans. This is the time of enslavement – the exercise of absolute power of one race of people over another. Where Blacks are bought, sold and owned as personal property and White people exert dominion over them and the fruits of their free labour.

**Book 2 - Freedom Bells are Ringing** set between the mid-1800s and 1900s is the book where, at first, hesitantly and cautiously the newly freed Enslaved, celebrate freedom only to realize that the ringing of the freedom bell was a hollow unfulfilled promise. In this book, we see the continuation of enslavement in other crueller ways. Slavery was perpetuated through the systems of segregation and Jim Crow. The book, celebrates the lives and struggles of stalwarts like Harriet Tubman, Robert Smalls, W.E.B Dubois, Frederick Douglass, Viola Desmond, Malcolm X and Martin Luther King Jr.

**Book 3 - Hidden in Plain Sight** explores systemic racism in the modern day. It describes yet another evolution of enslavement. All the old accoutrements, language, symbols and memories of the past have been challenged and some have been rooted out and destroyed. However, one mechanism is left to dismantle – systemic racism. It is the spectre of racism that is hidden in plain sight.

**Book 4 - A Companion Reader** is written as a companion to books 1 to 3 and allows the reader to read about the historical context without poetry. It references the poetry by book and according to chapter content.

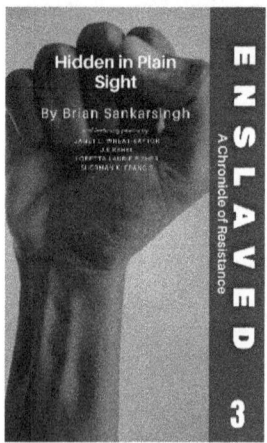
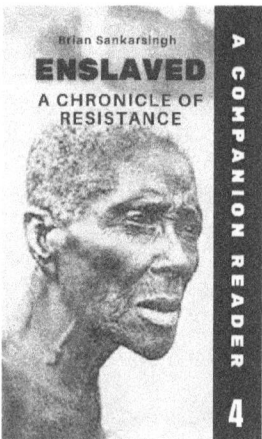

# Book 3
# HIDDEN IN PLAIN SIGHT

*Figure 1 - Hidden In Plain Sight*

# I am Jameila Alford

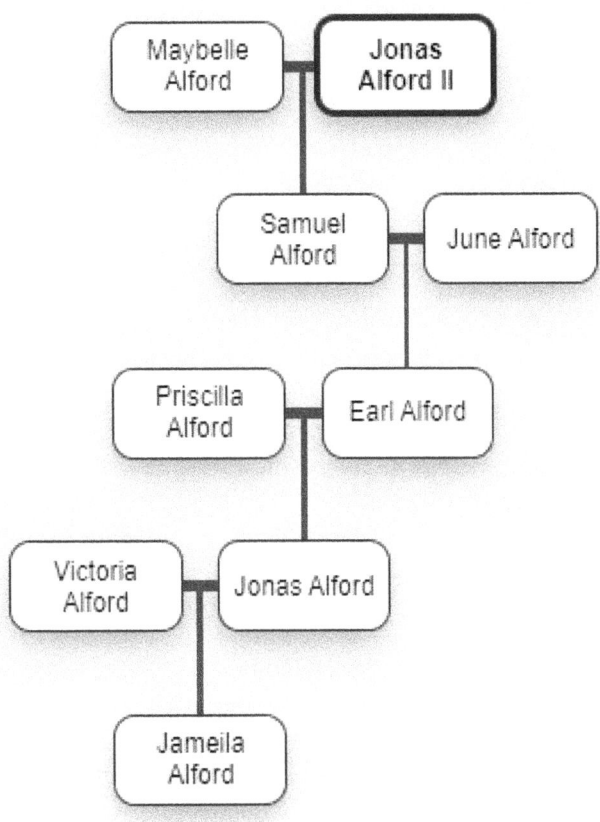

*Figure 2 - Mufa's Family Tree Pt 2*

Although separated from her ancestor Mufa by many generations, Jameila Alford knew about Nri since she was a child.

The refrain

"I am a child of the Kingdom of Nri,
We believe ALL men are born to be FREE.
This gift is granted by Chukwu to all,
That enter into Nri's great hall"

had been created into a carved ornate sign that hung in the front entryway of their home.

She knew how this refrain came to belong to her family and was very proud of it. It helped her in her darkest times and inspired her to be the best she could be. Jameila was a civil rights lawyer and activist, and she credited her family and a knowledge of their history as a part of her success.

Jameila understood the importance of family history and understood how the loss of it could destroy entire generations.

One small refrain, passed on in every generation
Providing inspiration, stability and direction
One small bit of history that would unite everyone
Past and future forming a connection

Helping each generation find their place in the world
Providing each person with an objective
That small bit of history so gently preserved
Was enough to provide an incentive

\*\*\*

## Setting the stage

Joe Feagin, in his book Racist America: Roots, Current Realities, and Future Reparations[ii] says

> *"Systemic racism includes the complex array of anti-Black practices, the unjustly gained political-economic power of White people, the continuing economic and other resource inequalities along racial lines, and the White racist ideologies and attitudes created to maintain and rationalize White privilege and power. Systemic here means that the core racist realities are manifested in each of society's major parts [...] the economy, politics, education, religion, the family reflects the fundamental reality of systemic racism."*

In Era 1, we witnessed the beginning of the trade of the enslaved. The theme was about one race exercising superiority and dominion over another. This was expressed in terms of humanity versus savages or sub-humans. White supremacy used religion, economics, and copious amounts of violence to position the White race as superior to all others. There was no need to be covert about this for it was the foundation upon which the entire trade of enslaved peoples was built.

Era 2, as Freedom bells were ringing, these assumptions of humanity were being directly challenged. White supremacy worked tirelessly to maintain its power and authority. It took steps to build barriers so that newly freed Blacks could not participate in many of the existing systems such as education, finance and wealth building, housing, media and communications, and health. It used existing legal systems and structures to ensure compliance and enacted laws when necessary. These barriers became the natural underpinning for Jim Crow and ultimately segregation. Separate but equal means nothing when there are substantial and noticeable differences between the "equals."

Black people continued to fight for true equality and ever so slowly something started happening. With every legal victory, every peaceful march and every push against the establishment, racism seemed to lose and disappear. They soon realised that it was not gone; instead of the overt racism they had experienced in the past, it became covert. To perpetuate itself, this covert racism embedded itself into all public institutions. For example, Blacks could go into a bank and open a bank account but would not get the type of service or be able to access bank resources that a White person would. Another example was that the fallacy promoted by the medical establishment that Blacks, especially Black women had a higher tolerance to pain[iii]

This racism wasn't just the result of the actions of one individual but were the accepted and often unspoken cultural and racial norms of the institution. In other words, it was systemic.

***

## Abolition: Disappeared Promises

Systemic racism did not just happen. It was conceived in the slavery's dying breath and sustained by a continued belief, that White supremacy was a God-given right. Like a vicious parasite it entrenched itself into every political decision, substituting good for bad at every turn.

In due time, this unconscious bias was embedded into corporate and government institutions affecting job opportunities, health and wellbeing, democratic rights, housing, wealth building and family life.

After the 'abolition of slavery' in Canada and the U.S.
Reparations were owed to Black people for being oppressed
But no justice for enslavement was never addressed
As the country was still run by colonial capitalists

There were empty promises and lip service that wouldn't stand
To atone for the kidnapping and genocide of generations of Africans
For inflicting such terrorist torture on humans and then decades beyond this
Not even one day in court for the Queen's minions; case dismissed

So, forty acres of land and even the mule were struck from the list
The state had no intention of allowing us any rights to insist
Colonizers pretended to wash their hands of being our enslaver
Quickly labelled us criminals, to continue building their empire faster!

Black people suddenly 'free' to work, yet not likely to be hired
Unless it's for labourious farm-work that White owners still desired
Many towns in the South ensured that actual by-laws be made
Stating Black women be offered jobs only as housekeeping maids

Cooks, baby-sitters, laundry workers, cleaners to keep up the shine
Choosing any other career path was an illegal chargeable crime
Finally ready for paid work because they had families to feed
Black men reduced to shoe-shine boys from 1900's to fifties
Constantly called out as perpetrators, and still kept in poverty
Colour coded criminalization: prison labour of these men used for free
Life sentences, yet still laboured to build buildings for our capital cities
Normalized incarceration was a way to steal our lives generationally
Through school-to-prison pipeline, we're funneled disproportionately
Targeted with trumped up sins of fathers passed down to sons' too easily

***

## Good news...Slavery's Abolished!

The abolition of slavery – what it must have meant to the enslaved who were fighting so hard against the yoke that lay heavily upon their necks. One imagines them beginning to dream of the possibility of a better future for the very first time in their lives.

Slavery's abolished!
We scream with a flourish!
Everyone under the sun
Is now as free as every other one
All of that shit we once believed, is now in the past
We kinda knew deep in our hearts, it wasn't going to last
Now, everybody's equal! We even wrote it down
Yes, everyone is equal; yellow, black or brown
Interracial marriages? Sure, we don't even care
Seek your fame and fortune; be a millionaire
Be a business owner. Be a movie star
You can live "the good life" with champagne and caviar
Celebrate our way of life, it's much better than the rest
Aren't you proud of all we've done? How much we have progressed?

\*\*\*

## ...No! You're wrong!

Draw a line from the Emancipation Proclamation to MLK Jr. speech "I have a Dream" however and one is left to wonder what's changed. Connecting MLK Jr.'s speech to our present day shows such minimal improvement that it's depressing.

No! You're wrong! Mistaken! We've not really been set free!
All that shit's still happening, in actuality
Physical chains have been removed but bound we still remain
You may argue otherwise, but it's a trick of legerdemain
The systems that govern us all are skewed to lighter skin
When we point out inequity, it's like a deadly sin
Someone has to prove your guilt, my innocence always questioned
Just my colour is enough to get arrested for possession
I must work twice as hard as you, to qualify for the same loan
You say you don't see colour, but you still act in monotone
If we point out inequality, you scream that ALL LIVES MATTER
In your race we've always been held back, our lives left

torn and tattered
We will not sing capitalisms' praise, that's not the freedom that we crave
The chains may not be around our necks, but we know that we're still slaves

\*\*\*

# A dream

Martin Luther King Jr.'s dream[iv] inspired many generations of people and continues to do so even now and while we have made strides in making it a reality, the journey is far from over.

He had a dream
A powerful lucid dream of unity and equality
This was no daydream
No reverie, musing or futile fantasy

And in that dream
Races saw each other as part of a human family
It's not weird or extreme
To wish for an end to hate and enmity

\*\*\*

## Three in One

First poem - Read the first lines of every stanza
Second poem – Read the second line of every stanza
Third poem – Read the entire poem

I've been called all those derogatory names before
None of those odious words come as a surprise

They all lie littered upon the dusty floor
Along with the prejudice and hate they symbolize

I will not let them bother me or wallow in rancour
Animosity does not scare me, I will not be victimized

Before picking up your hate again, I pray that you ensure
The result might not be what you expect, I ask that you think twice

Be certain that you are ready to deal with BIPOC espirit de corps
We will not deal in violence, but we won't compromise

We've had enough of hate and prejudice, we'd like to underscore
This is not meant to scare you, we don't mean to dramatize

***

# A book

Writing this book has been a labour of love for all the poets involved as evidenced by the poem below. The conversations that we had were often uncomfortable and stretching. The poet who contributed this poem, did not feel that, as a White woman, she was qualified to contribute to a book about enslavement. But we should not demonize our allies. Martin Luther King Jr. knew that, but somewhere along the way some of us have forgotten it.

I am contributing to writing a book
A book with 2 White authors and 3 Black authors
If I hadn't said that would anyone know?
Would anyone care?
Does anyone care?
Does this make a difference to a reader?
If it does – or even if it doesn't
It should make everyone want to read this book

It is a book of strength
Of tenacity
Of survival
Of hope
Of love

Put down the book you are reading now
And immerse yourself in the wonders of these words
Come out the other side
And tell me how you feel

\*\*\*

## What will tomorrow bring

Humans are a dichotomy. Our propensity for violence and brutality is only slightly overshadowed by our altruism and self-sacrifice. Often a neck-by-neck race, one wonders how we can be both with the same passion and fervour. Where do you see yourself in this paradigm?

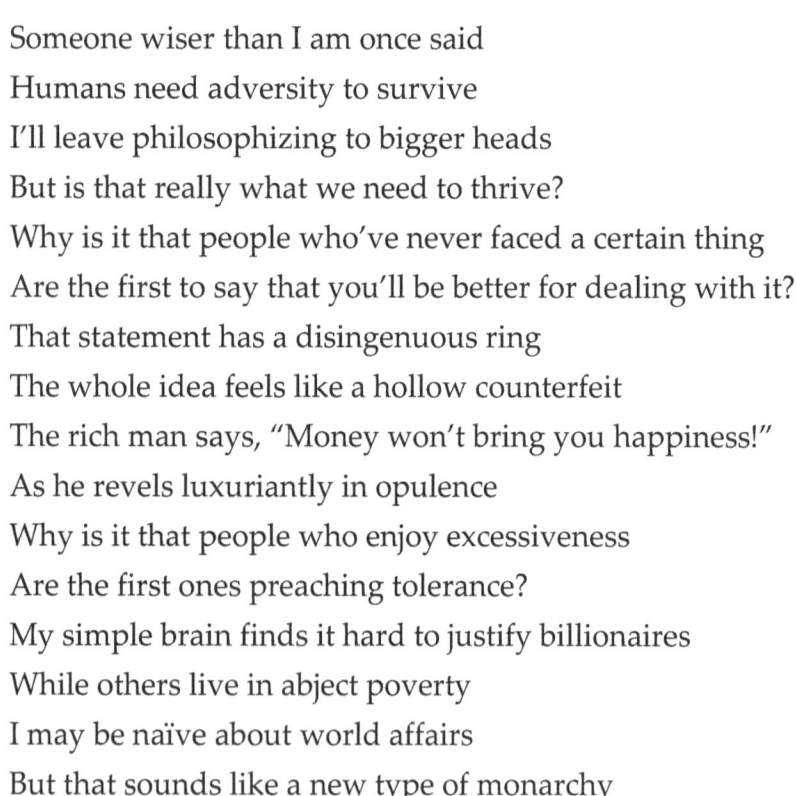

Someone wiser than I am once said
Humans need adversity to survive
I'll leave philosophizing to bigger heads
But is that really what we need to thrive?
Why is it that people who've never faced a certain thing
Are the first to say that you'll be better for dealing with it?
That statement has a disingenuous ring
The whole idea feels like a hollow counterfeit
The rich man says, "Money won't bring you happiness!"
As he revels luxuriantly in opulence
Why is it that people who enjoy excessiveness
Are the first ones preaching tolerance?
My simple brain finds it hard to justify billionaires
While others live in abject poverty
I may be naïve about world affairs
But that sounds like a new type of monarchy

CEOs who get paid three hundred percent more
Than the people they employ
One finds it difficult to have "esprit de corps"
When you're always someone else's whipping boy
Scraps to the starving can seem like a blessing
It may solve their immediate predicament
But how can humanity say it's progressing
In such a widely disparate environment
It's easy to hate when you're the dominant majority
To have a feeling of God-given entitlement
Flaunting authority and superiority
Every other race becomes merely transient
Religion says ignore your immediate circumstance
You'll get your reward when you die
I'm not entirely sold on that guidance
I'll let you guess about why
Work hard, pay your taxes and obey the law
Is the mantra we hear from the wealthy
Sounds really nice, if you're not starting out poor
Oh, but don't forget at least you're healthy
You may think my disillusionment is extreme
That I've lost my hold on reality
But even Martin Luther King once had a dream
So pardon my hyperbole
Unfortunately, I have no answers to provide
No easily workable resolution

But if we go on like this, I am terrified
Humanity will have no absolution
We will fail ourselves and our descendants
By maintaining this inequitable status quo
Leaving nothing but war and vengeance
A bleak and bloody tomorrow

***

# One Bad Apple

Some people say that there is no systemic racism. Many more would be at a loss to define systemic racism, preferring to blame the actions of a few bad people. The problem is however that there is too much evidence to the contrary[v]. The one bad apple[vi] response has been a go to argument for police in both Canada[vii] and the United States[viii], however there are many more layers to this poor defence.

There was once an apple in a barrel of more
This little apple was rotten to the core
Yet on the outside he appeared quite good
Bonded with his brothers in apple brotherhood

But something was happening way deep inside
Something pernicious, that rot couldn't hide
Just one black spot, there on his skin
A little indicator of the foulness within

Still his brother apples, ignored the small sign
Telling themselves everything will be forever fine
Their apple brotherhood survive under any pressure
If they could all, just stick together

## Hidden in Plain Sight

Yet our rotten apple, let's call him Andy
Shared his rottenness with his brother Sandy
Again, the other apples, said let's not have a quarrel
A few bad apples do not spoil the barrel

The farmer took one look at the barrel of apples
Picked at a few, he was checking for samples
He quickly realised the decay was widespread
Even though the apples still looked quite red

He knew that it was not about just one bad apple
That wasn't his reason for discarding the barrel
It was how easily the other apples accepted
Andy's rotten core, even after it was detected

When all apples choose to stick together
Just to protect a few rotten brothers
This type of rot, is not just endemic
Oh no my friend, that's what's called systemic

***

Brian Sankarsingh

## Jim Crow across the Eras: He Never Really Died

Systemic racism is not one size fits all. Its tacit acrimony affects different peoples in different ways. What is shared is the powerful negative and damaging effects it has on individuals and communities alike.

The bloody hard work of immigrant labourers and indentured service essential worker providers is still invisible
On properties WE were paid peanuts to build
We were deemed trespassers in the blink of an eye
Citizens have been legally allowed to stand their ground
But not if the citizen is non-White, Indigenous, Black or Brown
The darker skin you're in either you stand down or get shot down
Black workers owed unpaid wages has never yet been seen as a crime
Law makers announce everything is theirs, but if I'm BIPOC[ix] nothing is mine
Workers are trapped in poverty producing wealth and more wealth for the wealthy
That's the design

So many banks and bank loans for everyone to equally apply
But old Jim Crow rears his ugly head again and again to ensure we get denied
Such unfair laws are never admitted, instead it's said we never really tried
Wouldn't it be great to finally bury the carcass of old Jim Crow along with that zombie capitalism?
Usher in anti-racism and welcome #statusforall
Not just a futile hope or a fairy-tale wish;
This is the work of dedicated activists
Unlearning lies in order to decriminalize
Transforming violence into peace will take all of us working
But no longer divided

*\*\**

# How the West was raised

White supremacy and racism as so intricately bound together that it is impossible to speak about one without referring to the other. They both generally view BIPOC peoples as aggressive, repugnant and entitled. Systemic racism is more clandestine and covert. It furtively hides behind closed doors and is often experienced as only negative outcomes, by BIPOC peoples.

The West was raised on their addiction to a racist system
And a bag of media tricks full of prejudicial conjecturing
Truth gets locked down and buried since it might expose lies

White supremacists do not care who falls into despair
They aim to target and criminalize us exactly as they wish
Under their advance any slight chance for us must perish!

Refusing status for all, failing to have prisons abolished
Not even sheltered from grief - here stand our homeless!

Get over it and pull yourself up by the bootstraps they say
This cruel joke did not escape the notice even of MLK

He painstakingly explained how racist systems infect the air
then gets pumped directly into the veins of all children
since White supremacists don't care who falls into despair

Are any of us at this point still shocked and surprised
At the discrimination practiced from heartless race-based lies?
Some children grow up feeling free to be alive and safely thrive
While others get demonized and deemed to not deserve even smiles.
White supremacists have always known whose house to burn down
As the plan is to divide and destroy those who dare to care

\*\*\*

## 215 children

Many Canadians looked on in horror when the news broke of a gruesome discovery. The remains of two hundred and fifteen children were found buried at a former B.C. residential school. This grisly finding, only served to accentuate what First Nations, Indigenous and Metis people have been saying for decades. It's important for us to understand that what we perceive as colonialism against First Nations, Indigenous and Metis peoples in Canada, was a close cousin of racism that existed south of the Canadian border.

The horrors they had seen
The elders spoke of pain
Of children taken away
And never seen again

Years that should have been full of childish joy
And school years that should be fun
Were instead full of fear
And thoughts that could not be undone

## Hidden in Plain Sight

Unknown graves
Have recently been found
No one knows their contents
But numbers grew by leaps and bounds

Watching the elders talking
And seeing that they were so broken
Remembering all of the heartache
Of what has for so long been left unspoken

They said many prayers
On that hallowed ground
Praying for peace
For all who have been found

\*\*\*

# Jameila and Grandma Dot

As a child, Jameila was invited by a White friend to spend Christmas with her family. Little did she know how much this seemingly chance encounter would impact her life! In a little rural town, miles from nowhere on a farm, in the middle of winter, she tentatively entered Grandma Dot's kitchen. It was warm and welcoming, but not as much as the woman who ushered her in. Grandma Dot would go on to become a part of Jameila's extended family.

As a Black girl in a predominantly White city, Jameila was accustomed to negative experiences related to her race. But the welcome she received from Grandma Dot renewed her faith in humanity. She did not see Jameila's colour. She saw her humanness. We must hope that all humans may one day show that same ability. This is Jameila's recounting of what a profound impact Grandma Dot had on her life.

*This poem is written in dedication to Grandma Dot, in October 2021.*

## Hidden in Plain Sight

Her faced told a story of a life well lived
Each wrinkle, furrow and line bore witness
None but her knew what she'd survived
Nothing could diminish her light's brightness

She and her Valentine after the great war
Settled down to build the family ranch
Here, in what seemed like the middle of nowhere
Together they would make their stand

Even when she lost her husband, she still carried on
Mother and father to her family
All of life's chaos, she faced with calm
No complaint or theatricality

I remember our first meeting and her welcoming smile
"Any friend of my granddaughter is a friend of mine"
She didn't judge my colour or question my lifestyle
Thinking of it now, bring shivers to my spine

She saw only the person, not the colour or their race
All people were created equal in her eyes
She was the epitome of contentment and grace
With her there was no deceit or ill surprise

She learned to play computer solitaire
For her it was brand new
I asked "Grandma have you ever used a mouse?"
She replied, "No but I killed a few."

Granma Dot passed away; she was ninety-seven
Her loss was felt by all the lives she touched
She was indeed a precious gift from heaven
And we all miss her so much

***

## Oh Canada – Part One

Historian and poet, Afua Cooper describes slavery in Canada as one of Canada's best kept secrets[x]. However, slavery in Canada lasted over two hundred years. Black and Indigenous peoples suffered and died under the rule of Canadian enslavers. What might be even more shocking to hear is that although we often read about the Underground Railroad, going from South to North, there were times during Canadian slavery when the railroad went North to South.

If you believe Canada never had slavery
That escaped slaves came here to be free
Unfortunately, you are mistaken
Even here, Black freedom was not guaranteed
It was only until the first of August 1834
That slavery was illegal, under the law
But its absence would awaken
A new monster, rotten to the core

\*\*\*

## It's not all Black and White

In 2020, the Associated Press among many other news agencies made the decision to stop capitalizing the W in White when referring to race[xi]. This was an intentional change. They said for them, it was a necessary change.

White people often scream about BIPOC peoples challenging their language and their culture without taking the time to understand that much of that culture and even the language has been about oppressing BIPOC peoples.

But is it necessary to alienate all White people in a bid to punish the racists? Should we demonize the people who want to be our allies just because of the colour of their skin? Does that make us any better than them?

Does capitalization matter?
Or is this just lefty liberal irrationality
Maybe the question is would you rather...
...Be a good human or indulge your White supremacy

But is it White supremacy
If as your ally, I question why
Why do your thoughts go immediately to confederacy
How is that justified?

Is there no middle that we can meet
Instead of one side or the other
Surely this is true equality
When we truly see one another

\*\*\*

## A Strange Inconsistency

A paper titled The Pervasive Reality of Anti-Black Racism in Canada, The current state and what to do about it[xii] by Nan DasGupta, Vinay Shandal, Daniel Shadd, and Andrew Segal, in conjunction with CivicAction states: "Black workers are twice as likely as Asian workers and four times as likely as White workers to report experiencing racial discrimination in major decisions at workplaces in Canada." However, that not where the discrimination starts. Even getting that job can be a challenge for many Black people and People of Colour.

Seeking employment but being counted out in a certain way
Consistently and seemingly innocently.
You'd think HR might have noted my qualifications clearly
and that's why they would decide to interview me?
But after my interviews they're so quick to prophesy:
'Not a good fit; sorry, but you're over-qualified!'
Should my ability to do a job even better than expected be
Considered a good reason to say sorry and good-bye?

Interviewers use this 'over-qualified' claim to throw us aside
Straight into OW[1] where supposedly training is needed, right?
So many on OW [xiii] called unskilled, needing upgraded training Yet somehow, at the same time, we're over-qualified?

Employment agencies mention no such thing
It's quite the opposite that job counsellors are advising
Get more qualifications, education and experience to get in
That's the way of all job competitions we're trying to win

But then again, they also maintain innocently
It's illegal to discriminate based on the colour of one's skin
They claim that's the case, but the opposite is our reality
If we insist on the unfairness of this reality that's when the backlash from the system really begins

\*\*\*

---

[1] Ontario Works is a social service provided to unemployed workers

# Plantation Capitalism: A Bitter Sugar Addiction

The Trans-Atlantic Slavery Trade did not only chase after free labour. It also included other commodities like sugar. The planting, harvesting, and processing of sugar cane into sugar, played a large role in colonialists de-humanizing an entire race of humans from Africa.

First Europeans, then Americans fell headlong into this abusive practice of enslaving the African people for enormous profits. Sugar plantation owners used this enslaved labour to produce sugar as inexpensively as possible to improve their economy.

The result was inhumane conditions and continuous brutality for enslaved people on sugar plantations.

Enslaved people's labour and the rise of the western empire
Are tightly intertwined, and painfully so on one side
Generations of genocidal and torture-based labour
Forced on Africans by the White capitalists in favour
Leaves a terribly bitter after-taste lingering centuries later...

...Both sugar obsessions and racial tensions refuse to subside
But now is the crucial time for all humas to unite as allies and rise up against capitalist bosses who continue to utilize
Racialized people who are dying while serving the "civilized"

Learn the truth of the past that led to inequity today
Our children desperately need to know the truth anyway
Everyone's children...if there's to be hope for the future
Our children should not be deeply depressed but elated!
So children's history books will need to be updated
Although it's painful to see how much we were hated

Today, racial hatred hides much deeper under the surface
Having grown stronger roots even though it seems abated
Real empathy and real facts must be faced in history class
Plantation capitalism embedded now as much as in the past
Face it and work to erase it, so we can all move on at last

Except the ultra-rich elites in power do not drink to our health

Always scheming, in case we try to win back the common wealth
But we must because it was built by us and belongs to us - go figure
Elites always fight rather than give up this mighty addiction to sugar

\*\*\*

## Break the cycle

Racial prejudice and hate are a vicious cycle that can be passed down through entire generations. We hope and believe that the cycle can be broken but often it is so deeply ingrained in people that they say and do hateful things without even knowing it. In workplace and education environments, some Black people and people of colour have been accused covertly and overtly about their abilities. "You did this paper on your own? Impossible. You must have had help."

This can also be applied to the many public and corporate institutions that serve us. Their historical hate and prejudice are buried so deeply yet still affects the service.

This poem is written in a cycle as witness to the cycle of racial prejudice. The second line of the first stanza becomes the first line of the second. The third line of the second becomes the first line of the third. But breaking the cycle, the third line of the third stanza becomes the first line of the fourth, which finally ends with the first line of the first stanza.

This symbolizes breaking the cycle of hate and starting over with hope.

I put my life into your hands, and hope that you will see
The humanity within me and not the colour of my skin
That doesn't always happen, though you may disagree
Sometimes your racist attitude lies hidden deep within

The humanity within me and not the colour of my skin
Should dictate the way you treat and interact with me
My colour on the outside has become a familial sin
Sadly, this is my current truth and reality

My colour on the outside has become a familial sin
I often wonder if your hate is hereditary
Racial prejudice and hate are wars no one ever wins
Its weight is too much for humanity to carry

Racial prejudice and hate are wars no one ever wins
Everyone will bear the scars of hate to a particular degree
They remain forever in our minds and on our skins
I put my life into your hands, and hope that you will see

***

## Oh Canada – Part Two

Many Canadians would balk at the mention of racism in Canada[xiv]. They believe that this is a topic more suited for our Southern neighbours. Those same Canadians also probably don't know that Canadians were also enslavers. Or that Canada, in as late as the Twentieth Century, had immigration policies that discriminated against allowing non-European immigrants into the country.

These racist attitudes do not simply disappear. Often, they entrench themselves deeply into communities, government and corporate organizations.

On the surface everything seems serene,
people focused on altruism
But tease apart the societal fabric and
you'd be sure to find racism
What looked so beautiful from the front,
multitudinous race and colour
When you see its ugly underbelly, you'll
recoil in horror

Governments may make it illegal to be
racist or discriminate
Yet they cannot change what's in the hearts of
those that choose to hate
Social programs, education, punishment for racial
prejudice and intolerance
Helps to make many feel that systemic
racism is merely an aberrance, but
Politics, law enforcement, healthcare,
finance and education
All have seen their fair share of
racial discrimination
That's why we say its systemic because it
is embedded within our institutions
This is the problem we must address and
together find solutions

But to begin this difficult journey, we must
accept the reality
That being White in Canada comes with
certain guarantees
One that is not necessarily had, by Black people
and People of Colour
Even though on the surface it may appear that
they're comfortable with the culture

A White politician saying that they believe
systemic racism no longer exists
Means they are not listening to all their constituents
and important messages were missed
I beg you listen my fellow Canadian don't be
so quick to celebrate
There is still quite a lot of work for us to do to
be rid of racial hate

*\*\**

## Not alone

Each line in this poem stands witness to a White person's journey. The realization that things were not what they seemed. That systemic racism was real even though a White person will never experience it. The intent is not to make people feel guilty, but for people to understand that there are so many other levers and pressures at play.

Sometimes I am ashamed...
   ...Ashamed of being White
   ...Ashamed of White slave masters
   ...Ashamed at others judging someone by their colour
   ...Ashamed that it took so long to open my eyes to atrocities

I wonder why
   ...Why some White people feel that a person of any other colour should be victimized
   ...Why they should be treated differently
   ...Why – just why?

Today I feel strength
   ...Strength to stand up for the pain others have been through

...Strength to put into words the shame we feel
...Strength to help write a book so others can read
...and react
...Strength to tell others that they are not alone

***

## Still Tricked: Justice is M.I.A[2].

Once promised 40 acres and a mule, historically, Black people have been tricked, disenfranchised and cheated of the fruits of their labour. In 2020, the Canadian government reached a $31-billion settlement to compensate indigenous children and families harmed by discriminatory underfunding of the child welfare system on First Nations reservations[xv]. These are just some of the ways BIPOC peoples have suffered – and continue to suffer - from racism and systemic racism.

North American and International students so saddled with debt because somebody lied
Racialized workers the first to perish in plagues but deemed by government as fine
Financial justice
Health justice
Racial justice
Housing justice
Climate justice
#justice4workers
Just plain old justice is all missing in action
Do you see the common denominator of this infraction?

---

[2] Missing in action

Justice was never even intended
We've been so slickly tricked
It's the wealthy elite alone who always benefit
Adding to their privilege

Calling us inferior and unskilled and barely deserving.
We must stand up to resist abuse
Refuse to stay subservient
They claim we're not equal to them and
try to justify police violence

Is it a great multicultural system? You want anything just work hard?
As if we have not been working very hard here for generations!
Without fair compensation, paid sick days, or any reparations!

If we make any $$ it gets spent all on rent and in their super-stores
Unless we bring money we're only 'allowed' to enter through back doors

Who knows when this global pandemic of capitalism ends
Along with all its evil side-effects intensifying unfair trends

Unite against racist capitalism and save the earth from being destroyed
We need African and Indigenous wisdom for all justice to be restored!

***

## The Black in BIPOC

Canada's Black populations suffer tremendously from systemic oppression at all levels. This includes, but is not limited to, more negative education outcomes, reduced likelihood of finding a job, diminished opportunities for career progression, inferior healthcare including mental health and wellbeing and significantly more negative outcomes from police interactions[xvi].

Look at me!
Stop, and
Look. At. Me!

My black skin is hidden
In the shadows of your apathy
You look through me
With counterfeit sacrosanctity
I don't want any of that
Enough with rationalization
Do something about it
We're tired of this inaction
We're not just an affirmative action
Waiting for a handout
There is a moral imperative

To figure this thing out
I scream that Black Lives Matter
Because Black lives are in jeopardy
Your response of all lives matter is
A testament to your insincerity
Walls always appear in front of me
Hidden in plain sight, forever
Trapped in your free society
This will no longer suffice
For I will force you to

Look at me!
Stop, and
Look. At. Me!

\*\*\*

## The Indigenous in BIPOC

First Nations, Indigenous and Metis peoples in Canada have suffered and continue to suffer greatly from systemic racism. There are still many Indigenous communities that do not have clean fresh drinking water.

It is critically important for EVERY Canadian – not of First Nations, Inuit and Metis descent - to recognize that they are Settlers in Canada. A settler is someone who has migrated to and established a permanent residence somewhere else. This is often understood within the context of colonization but within the context of Truth and Reconciliation applies to all immigrants.

I did not come here to conquer or subjugate
I came seeking refuge and asylum
All I sought was sanctuary
A chance to be "Canadian"

But what of those who came before
Who came to colonize and occupy
Should I be grateful to them for creating
A place where I could find safety?

And what of those who
Roamed these lands before us all?
Who loved these lands before we did?
Creating the paths that we now tread?

Can I ignore the mournful cries?
Of the First Peoples who walked upon this land
If the violence visited upon their lives
Wasn't done by my ancestor's hand

Can I enjoy the benefits of colonization?
Without the brutal violence of its birth
Is my own hand not equally stained?
From the theft of life, of land and hearth
Why should I care to fight for this?
For something I did not even cause
Can I not just simply live my life?
And on special days reflect and pause?

In truth, I am also a settler
And I benefit from that past trauma
Its fabric is interwoven in my own life
A part of the Indigenous diorama

If I don't try to build relationships
Address the wrongs that they were dealt
Am I not just as complicit?
In violating the treaty of the two-row wampum belt?

There is no doubt upon my mind
I owe a debt to my Indigenous family
As surely as I sit upon this land
I cannot adopt a stance of neutrality

Each day I must do my part to make amends
If our collective lives are to be worthwhile
Acknowledge the past and change the future
Is one way for me to reconcile

To continue living on Turtle Island
I must pledge to challenge my worldview
To explore, appreciate and understand
The true meaning of two canoes

***

## The People of Colour in BIPOC

One of the reasons for the term BIPOC where Black and Indigenous peoples have been highlighted, is because of the specificity of the relationship these peoples have with White supremacy.

According to the Canadian Race Relations Foundation, People of Colour is "a term which applies to non-White racial or ethnic groups; generally used by racialized peoples as an alternative to the term visible minority.[xvii]"

The fact is my friend, here in North America
If you're not White, you're Black
This construct was superficially created
To allow dominion and control
Using violence and religion
To create a stranglehold
So that one race could claim supremacy
Rule completely above all others
A zealous form of pedigree
Of White over any other colour
A society was created
To force minorities
To serve the White colonial enslavers

And accept their authority

Of course, this time is long gone
But sadly, change is slow to come
If you're Black, Indigenous or Brown
Your life generally has lower outcomes
Whether it's in education
Finance or your career
You will probably face stagnation
Permanently stuck in your first gear
That's if you're not racially profiled
In an encounter with police
For being at the right place at the right time
Your colour is your motif

\*\*\*

## Rotten House

Charity begins at home. So does racists ideology. Do you know someone who lives in a rotten house?

In his house a sense of morality was lost
Take matters in your own hands at any cost
At seventeen you can do as you will
The consequences of your choices, we'll pay the bill
He learnt to disregard the sanctity of life and respect for all humanity
And to respect only those who looked the same with matching ideologies
His undisciplined life almost cost him his head
But that's coming from a home where the love for equality is dead

We've heard many stories about the men in blue
Much of what's going on in their house is true
The implementation of the law should be without partiality
How one is treated, colour normally determines the severity
If your skin takes a certain shade, you're given a pass
And these cues trickle down from the top brass

## Hidden in Plain Sight

The general rule of this house is racial profiling
Stop, frisk and handcuff regardless of what you're driving
The house of justice, an artifact from the same mold
More criminals on the bench than those in the hold
The mercy seat has been packed with selective vision
Status and dollar signs recognized, all others receive derision
Total disparity in this profession, an office that requires veneration
The evidence of injustice goes without condemnation
A brother of colour with a gun, could be sentenced for life
His Caucasian neighbor with a gun is sent home to sleep with his wife

The house of laws, built with bricks from the same factory
Its members easily switch sides, it's documented in history
To get anything done there, some say it's a dream
Little do they know, they all play on the same team
Hence common-sense legislation is never enacted
And their political gestures are only to keep you attracted
The sincere ones are either silenced or punished
Play the game to keep your seat, or your career is finished

Is your house teaching to treat all with impartiality?
That a man is a man irrespective of his colour or nationality?

Discrimination should be looked upon with revulsion
Demonstrated in your speech, your deportment and your actions
Those sown seeds of hate, its roots are not that convoluted
When seen in your progeny carefully have them uprooted
Then this vicious cycle can envision and end
And your house a refuge the marginalized can depend
Between wage theft and tax evasion, ultra-rich head upward

\*\*\*

## Amassing Wealth is not Common Wealth

For BIPOC peoples, wealth does not level the playing field. That's because you see their skin colour before you see their wallet. Nevertheless, poverty is a prison that destroys BIPOC families and access to a fair living wage and affordable living conditions can make a difference.

Between wage theft and tax evasion, ultra-rich head upward
While slickly groomed high-end lawyer/politicians ensure
Financial loopholes created just for them are tightly secured
These high-class perks are here, and also overseas, but mum's the word

Shhh! Money-laundering; it's the neatest crime in the West
But a crime's not a crime when it's just "Business at its Best"
Stealing so much from our economy, they will never confess

Boggles the mind how elites flipped the script on crime
They're not compelled to admit to it, or return one thin dime

But this truth is yet to be reported in The N.Y. Times
Stocks and bonds enrich the elite on Bay and Wall Street
Resulting in untold plethora of assets multiplied
By the thieving-est colonialist capitalist minds

But Pandora's secret got out, over 80 billion is stashed
Snowbirds luxuriate in her embrace each winter en-masse
Even strict COVID-19 rules could not keep the jet-set back
Hoping not to be recognized at the airport in cheap masks!
Elites have many rules for the poor; less for VIP/diplomats
Rules that elites quietly break regularly at home and abroad
But constantly accuse the working-class of fraud
This complete hypocrisy is more than just odd!
Routinely make workers work extra, but not pay wages fairly
Their way of pushing us down; that's what 'oppression' means
Only partial wages are the bosses' brilliant malignant scheme
Withholding pay from workers to shrink our financial dreams

But their financial dreams escaped all the cages to freely fly
Over $80 billion: the jackpot from elite evaders at tax time
…plus $933 million: the lucrative booty of wage theft crime

amounts to amassing amazing wealth from their workers by devious design.
Wealth created by us; stolen/hoarded only for elite progeny
Wealth that's originally and rightfully working-class property
Wealth ripped from workers, the backbone of our economy
Please, please bring back Pandora's wealth from over the sea
Back to working-class wallets of those who built this country

Elite upper-class imperialists think that they built this country
They didn't; they stole it and continue to break every treaty
Making no laws to stop themselves from being so greedy
Or to force themselves to have any kind of accountability
Or protect the working class they pretend to love so much
at Voting time, elite politicians cannot promise enough
But that won't stop them from trying with more lying
since siphoning the wealth off our cheques is never enough?!

People need to find comrades who'll unite and empower us
to deliver a collective push-back and say enough IS enough!
Colonizers' claim to fame is time and again their racist refrain that keeps them plundering land as if it's their sole domain
But the people won't stop our resistance to being enslaved!

\*\*\*

## Oh Canada – Part Three

Oh! Canada
Please listen carefully, I have something to say
I'm sorry ahead of time, if it causes some dismay
There is a hidden underbelly of racial prejudice
It's often passive aggressive and insidious

Oh. Canada
Social media fuels the fire of race, hate and bigotry
Because people feel, they have a certain anonymity
I can tell you about it, I've had it happen to me
Ask any BIPOC person, they might have the same story

Oh. Canada
Please don't take this personally, I only speak honestly
I don't intend to make a scene, or cause hostility
You may have heard a racial slur, from friend or family
But if you did not speak up, then that's a tragedy

Oh. Canada
BIPOC Peoples depend on you to be a good ally
Otherwise, some people just see us as the bad guy
Canada's strength is built upon its diversity
So let us stand against hate and do so purposefully

      \*\*\*

## Sinful Fraternization

The American First Amendment speaks about the separation of church and state. In Canada, although it is not explicitly stated, its importance is understood and followed in most provinces. There is a lot of historical precedence on the ills of a political-religion regime yet still many power-hungry people try to combine them to create and consummate their rule. Whenever this occurs, minorities, people of races other than the dominant, people who are seen as "other" are the first to suffer.

Politics and Religion should never mix, we know, it's a fact
They're both systems of control and only opposites attract

Neither are perfect, both have their own deficiencies
Both can be easily railroaded by eccentric personalities

Using one to bolster the other, is mixing fire with oil
Igniting a conflagration, that leaves nothing unspoiled

Time and again we've seen it, throughout our history
Yet time and time again we seek their combined toxicity

The problem with Religion, is that they want us to trust
That they alone have access to a celestial being's truth

We must subject ourselves to their divine-led instruction
Any other path we choose, will lead only to destruction

Acts of cruelty, hate and spite, if done in their god's name
Do not count as sinful, you are clear of blame and shame

This means a religion, once based on love and forgiveness
Can quickly lose sight of it all, and become a big business

Catering instead to the fanciful whims of powerful elites
More interested in Us vs. Them no longer seeking peace

Now, mix that with the added power of political regime
Suddenly it morphs into the narcissist's wet dream

***

Hidden in Plain Sight

# Part 1 - Female Black Achievers Take On The World

Wilma Rudolph[xviii] was an Olympic athlete. Sounds simple enough. Until you know that it was 1956, that Wilma was a Black woman and when she was young, she was sick and had to wear a brace on her left leg. Sounds like someone worth celebrating? Have you ever heard of her?

This poem will introduce two unassuming characters, and each has a unique and entirely different story
Yet both girls experienced Olympic success in all its' glory
At a time when African Americans endured sanctioned racism sorely

One Olympian you may have heard of if you're from U.S. and one you might not
But whatever their journey to win gold medals must have taken quite a lot
A lot of practice, pain, sacrifice, determination, and talent you name it
Personal achievements outside of the Olympics, they can also claim it

Absolutely nothing came easy for any Black people in Southern U.S.
So how in heaven's name did these Black female teenagers from the Jim Crow era become empowered to beat everyone's best?!

Their best ended up winning them the highest awards among the greatest Olympic competitors from across the entire globe
Yet these girls' families were scarred by deep racial abuse and ignored
They managed the impossible and found strength so many could barely afford

What I think they bought into it was tons of extreme self-determination
that's the first hurdle before thinking of winning medals for their nation

Meet young Wilma Rudolph! if you don't know her, her story's not folklore
You'll be gasping and cheering in utter amazement, I'm pretty sure

As a child she was stricken with polio and doctors said in her case
Wilma would not walk on her own, due to weakness she needed a brace

Leg braces she wore from age 6-12. But young Wilma was never alone
Struggling to overcome day to day she had 21 siblings cheering her on

Hoping she'd walk they never imagined Wilma winning any top prize
But they were familiar with the determination shining brightly in her eyes!

Long before becoming champion her struggles to recover strengthened her legs but it especially strengthened her resolve to survive
and her strength of character grew from the inside.
In spite of her fragile health, the doc's prognosis, and her petite size.

Track and field was 2nd choice; she wished basketball had been allowed

But recruited by an Olympic track coach who knew Wilma would do well
Wilma's lion-sized spirit paired nicely with the grace of a 'black gazelle'

That's what many fans called her as the only Black female in her field
She'd been called derogatory things, but to insults she didn't intend to yield

She took the lead and trained constantly; people were in awe of her ability Scarcely believing she was the same child struck with a physical disability!
As for Olympic Gold medals, Wilma Rudolph went on to win at least three defying her serious prognosis and also defying her socio-economic reality.

The entire world was awe-struck by this African American teen!
Had we ever seen anyone who was so determined to win
Wilma was a sheer force of strength and beauty with a big dash of miracles
So gracefully mixed in!
Way beyond all the bets against her, Wilma Rudolph would win

Wilma did not actually retire, but
Worked as a track coach at her university
Thanked her parents and all her siblings for being her #1 fans and family

Many see Wilma Rudolph's remarkable wins and say 'that's what I need!'
An iron will to act daily to achieve something that is an impossibility!

Every Olympic athlete gives it their all but Wilma Rudolph also captured the hearts of all

***

## Part 2 - Female Black Achievers Take On The World

Although racism and bias tried, they could never overshadow Wyomia Tyus's brilliance in sport, and they cannot take away from her achievements.

How is it that well past the time this former Olympic teen conquered the scene
She didn't feel like it was a big deal to publish her amazing memoir until 2018?
For those who didn't know, we're glad she did: "Tigerbelle: The Wyomia Tyus Story" All about her track and field excellence and this African Americans' rise to Olympic glory!
While Wilma's unique style saw her hailed as the 'Black Gazelle';
Wyomia's athletic strength saw her rushing in like a 'Tigerbelle'
Racing hot on her heels, Wyomia equaled Wilma's world record in track and field.
The only girl in her family with 3 older brothers, Wyomia was never one to yield
Her sharecropper Pa shared a hard truth: 'work at least twice as hard as anyone'

Working on a farm in Griffin, Georgia, she didn't feel free, but she felt born to run!
Dairy farm life was incredibly hard, then things got even worse when her Pa died
The poor family barely endured, but Wyomia's skill became well-known and bona fide
So, the same coach who'd trained Wilma Rudolph, soon stood by Wyomia's side
Urging her to get even stronger, she gained confidence to take the Olympics on
That world stage where athletes trained at least 'twice as hard' as everyone'!

Displaying super-athletic prowess won Wyomia one Silver medal, plus three Gold!!!
Her success dismissed by a press not pleased to admit Black excellence exists for the entire world to behold!
Her stellar achievements weren't celebrated widely by media, but down-played
At a time in history where society seriously wanted to see her only as a maid!
This did not stop Wyomia. Even after the Olympics she won many more races!
Note: It was Wyomia Tyus who first won two consecutive Gold Medals in '64 and '68

Nothing could stop this African American female from becoming an Olympic Great!

Wyomia was accustomed to repeatedly achieving her very best in every game

Her achievements and perseverance inspire our Black female Olympians up to today

Wyomia Tyus! So glad the world knows your name and your claim to excellence and fame!

\*\*\*

## Part 1 – Symbols

There is a debate on whether Confederate symbols should be removed or not[xix]. Southern states seceded from the Union to protect their way of life. This included enslaving human beings. They lost the Civil War battle, but would win the war for continued enslavement. To do this, they flexed their political and financial muscle in government and business to ensure that certain aspects of enslavement would remain legal. Now as many empowered BIPOC peoples demand the removal of what they perceive as symbols of hate and oppression this is what they're told.

Don't tell me to take down those statutes and effigies
They remind me of my ancestors and my family history
It's important to commemorate our country's past
We're a beacon to the world and will never be surpassed

Sure, I know the Confederates did not win the Civil war
A dark stain on our history that we must all endure
But I'll be damned if I let you blackwash my history
With your revisionist politically correct toxicity

\*\*\*

# Random acts of Racism

Many people's understanding of racism is most often limited to stark, and often violent acts. The murder of George Floyd, Breonna Taylor and many more. However, BIPOC peoples face daily instances of racism that can deeply affect them. We must all be empowered to call out these random acts of racism without being called "snowflake," "pinky liberal" or being told to "grow up" or "take it like a man!" These responses serve only to make random acts of racism even more spiteful and malicious.

What's more, these acts can be institutionalized – think of the store employee who follows the young Black man around because he is stereotyped as being a criminal or a thief.

I don't know you brother, but I'll call you 'Brother Z'
I happened to witness you being quickly but viciously
Cut down and burned by such a damning remark
Aimed by a stranger like an ugly poison dart
And this kind of invective never misses the mark
Astounding assumptions in a crowded mall parking lot
I call you Brother Z because I know that shit hurts a lot!
So, you observed road rules while driving

The Most Incredible Car I have ever seen!!
Everyone's eyes popped; like something out of a future 'zine
We all turned to look at your car as you peacefully drove by
'A famous sports athlete celebrity?'
But it was not me entertaining any of that conjecture
It was all about the glorious vehicle, it was so spectacular!
But maybe it's exactly what some White people are groomed to do
When expressly trained to believe their assumptions of 'you'
Informed by prejudice, their conjectures are presumed true:
Far and Wide
Informed through centuries of racial hatred and lies

Whereas the reality of it was there was one human being who skillfully controlled a truly beautiful car going by
But that's not at all what an impudent person was seeing:
"How many drugs didja hafta sell to buy that?!" she screamed!

The racist question was trotted out with privileged impunity
It was a beautiful day before; but now it was faded beauty
and suddenly, a rotten cloud hung over the whole place
This cold-hearted White female felt so entirely safe
to actually yell with her hands cupped around her face

Why was she compelled by a need to maximize her voice?
Likely to ensure we all heard, as if she left us a choice
I was walking right beside her car when she jumped out
to abruptly shout!
I jumped like everyone else within range of her
and my psyche silently signaled 'Fire!' and 'Danger!'
It was the content not the volume that made me feel so sick
How easy it is to imagine how you, Brother Z, felt about this
Simply driving in your own town minding your own business

Yet it's as if certain males can't proudly show off their cars
in the same way all top-line vehicles are admired like stars
So, you got hit with racist criminalization! Random, or is it?
I know it was shameful, disheartening, and we're sick of it!
She didn't call the cops I think but still exhausting, and not new

What she yelled at you, Brother Z, was meant to harm you!
It was meant to be racist, mean, and rhetorical
And ohh so familiar, along the lines of historical
After her unprovoked outburst I was close enough to observe
She smirked so proudly like she delivered what was deserved
She got quickly back into her car, then her partner drove off
No physical harm done, no visible injury, and no fatal shot
And…
No way to prove or measure all of the painful emotional cost

*\*\**

## Part 2 – Symbols

In their daily life, BIPOC peoples continue to encounter systemic racism at every level. However, having the symbols of the philosophy and way of life that enslaved their ancestors and subjugated them to all manner of violence and atrocities is reprehensible. Past trauma can negatively affect physical and mental health.[xx] This happens, not just for the person who experienced this, but it is also intergenerational.

This is not a demand to destroy these symbols. The horrific acts they represent need to be remembered and understood – but they do not belong in public spaces!

Symbols are a reminder of things we regret we lost
They connect us to key moments in our lives
But there comes a time, when we must question the cost
Why those symbols were kept in our archives

Symbols that are divisive, ones rooted in greed and hate
Have no place in our collective mind
If they caused pain to others, how can we celebrate
Something that would make another feel maligned

Sure, we must know our history, so that it's not repeated
And slavery is wickedness incarnate
Its shameful immorality should never be permitted
This is the cause for which we advocate

A museum is the place for these reminders of slavery
To teach what they are and what they mean
Having them in public, is so unsavoury
An act that is bordering on the obscene

\*\*\*

# Hidden in Plain Sight

It is quite interesting to listen to White people tell Black people and People of Colour that the systems that we must all interact with are working just fine. Of course, they are – if you're White. Education, Finance, Real estate, Banking, Voting, Justice, Policing and many more were all created to serve the needs of the White population. For many years access to these institutions and the services they provided were only afforded to White people. Black people and People of Colour got services after the fact and even then, were discriminated against. Often this discrimination was represented by actual policies but over time, they became so ingrained and embedded into the institutions that it was the way they did business.

This is what is meant by systemic racism. The fact that even today, young Black women in University are being accused of having help to do a paper because of its deep intellectual insight. Black women and women of colour are believed to have a higher pain threshold and thus don't receive the same medical care and attention. Black men are refused medical attention, because it is believed they are just trying to get drugs. First Nations peoples are discriminated against with some communities not even having access to clean water. Indigenous Peoples, Black people and People of Colour are discriminated against by police. Of course, these things are reported on, but they continue to happen. Why? Because they're hidden in plain sight.

Where is our big dipper, to keep us on the right path
As we navigate the wilderness we created
How do we avoid our homegrown wrath
To escape from the milieu of hatred

Prizing individuality above everything else
Unintentionally creating a narcissistic world
Simple life, now made unnecessarily complex
Rushing to the edge of the abyss undeterred

Everyone's an expert and we're all talking heads
Being an influencer is the Holy Grail
Concerned with following the latest trends
Good judgement no longer prevails

Karens, Stacys and Chads have their idiosyncrasies
While everyone else struggles to find meaning
Black Lives Matter fighting racism and bigotry
Political Left and Right only screaming

To hell in a handbasket seems like our demise
If we choose to continue this trajectory
Religious perversions in angelic disguise
The equivalent of a societal frontal lobotomy

Amidst all this clamour and dystopian noise
Every person fighting for their relevance
Is the heart-breaking sound of the oppressed voice
Challenging those with cognitive dissonance

When a group of people share a societal benefit
That is only earned through birth
This can be historically supremacist
It distorts what others see as their own worth

Systems created to serve a particular race
In many ways becomes a birthright
That's the reason many feel so displaced
By systemic racism hidden in plain sight

***

## Systemic Change

Often it can be challenging for a White person to understand systemic racism. They look to their own experiences interacting with police, education, the law and justice systems, real estate and so on, and they see no problem with it. Exactly! These systems were designed for them, by them and with them. Of course, it works well in their experience. This is the first step to a White person understanding systemic racism.

If you think that black is bad,
Then you need to hear my words
Black's the colour of my skin
Not the colour of a heart
What you think you see without
This is not the same within
You say you want equality
And get angry when I disagree
How can we be equal when
I'm not a part of this system?
When you think you know my pain
You may have to think again
For generations, you enriched your lives
On the backs of nameless slaves

Building systems to serve your needs
Using bondage to fuel your greed
You think these systems still don't exist
I'm here to tell you they still persist
I'm treated with disdain or fear
From financial systems to healthcare
Systems created to serve the master
Tend to treat me like a gangster
You need the drug, I am addicted
You get a warning, I am convicted
Don't be angry when I try to dismantle
Systems created to keep me shackled
Enjoying the fruits of my ancestors' labour
In no way makes me into a traitor
Come join me in this radical movement
Together let us make a statement

\*\*\*

## Documented Facts

A very well-known celebrity said *"When you hear about slavery for 400 years. For 400 years? That sounds like a choice. You were there for 400 years, and it is all of y'all?"* Anyone who took the time to read history would know that the enslaved did not just lie there and accept their fate. What stopped them? Organized systems! Systems created to ensure compliance. Systems created to catch runaways and make examples of them. Systems designed to maintain law and order. Systems that, for the most part, remained in place for many hundreds of years. Many of those systems that still exist in some shape or form today.

This is the reality of systemic racism.

Here are some more of this systems' strangely twisted facts:
We vote in politicians, fund their campaigns, and pay our taxes
for them to protect the working classes from greedy fascists
But if systems were not so biased with unfair policies and inequities

no one would even need assistance, or any of these charities!
Registered charities create more untold wealth for the rich
Banks use our life savings to grow a money-laundered glitch
where off-shore accounts of high officials hide untold billion$$
Cash disappeared from the Cdn economy and sorely missed
along with the old age pensions of citizens, and our E.I. benefits
These high officials? Namely our not so honourable politicians
But we just keep circuitously voting the same parties in
Why do we keep on giving them a free pass?
Time after time they've never protected the working class
Capitalist foxes are in charge of guarding the hen-house!
Time to stop government elite from letting big business enslave us!
Legislating gig work so that workers' have no protections
It's back to slavery days. What's wrong with this picture?
The whole script has been flipped and it has twisted society

Since "peace officers" do not offer peace -- only brutality!
None of this is mere conjecture, but don't take it from me
Check out the daily news, or a CBC documentary

\*\*\*

## Part I - I wish I were Black

In 1988, Peggy McIntosh published a paper titled White Privilege: Unpacking the Invisible Knapsack[xxi]. In this paper she defines the concept of White privilege with many concrete and powerful examples. At that time, its simplicity was profound and applicable.

However, over time many people reason that the playing field has been equalized and these inequalities no longer exist. Furthermore, they explain, we are so far away from slavery, desegregation and Jim Crow that these no longer hold sway on our thoughts and beliefs.

Is this true?

Is White privilege a thing of the past?

How come you're complaining about the lack of equality when I see many Black people doing so much better than me?

You have organizations with only people from your race, but if I were to do that it would be seen as a disgrace

There are things that you can say and do that if I ever were to attempt, the court of public opinion would hold me in contempt

I often hear you talking about my White privilege, but I must admit I don't feel like I have an advantage

I'm suffering the same as you in many ways its worse, but I still hear you complaining that your black skin can be a curse

I grew up in poverty and worked hard for everything I earned, never did I once complain, I did what had to be done

It often feels like my White race is constantly under attack so it's really weird to hear you speak about the negative experience of being Black

\*\*\*

## Part II – You have no idea what you're talking about

The word privilege means a special advantage or immunity or benefit not enjoyed by all; a right reserved exclusively by a particular person or group. In an early post-slavery world this White privilege was very obvious and observable. Even the lowest, poorest, meanest, dirtiest White person was considered superior to a Black man or a person of colour.

As time went on and Black people and People of Colour fought for their civil rights, they slowly began to claim territory once the sole habitation of White people. The right to equal transportation; the right to an education; the right to health and wellbeing; the right to good and affordable housing; the right to vote and so on.

This journey, however, is long and difficult. With each legal victory the discrimination DID NOT disappear. Instead, it went underground and resurfaced in other ways. Though not as observable, their malevolence was still palpable.

We don't disagree that many things have progressed; since the days of slavery when Black people were oppressed;

We've fought so very hard for the rights and freedoms we now have under the law; many lost their lives for this and their families so much more

When you speak about personal trauma affecting many generations on; this is also true for us, but for us it's still not gone

It was not just one of us who endured the trauma and agony; it was our entire race that faced this tragedy

Then to be constantly reminded of the pain and anguish our ancestors had to bear; through flags and historical monuments you celebrate without a care

So be careful what you wish for without fully understanding what we face; it may appear like we're okay, but your racism didn't just go away

\*\*\*

## Part III – And I'm not sorry to tell you so

Cory Collins in his paper, "What is White Privilege, Really?"[xxii] writes about the evolution of White privilege in today's "woke" society. In part he says "White privilege is not the assumption that everything a White person has accomplished is unearned; most White people who have reached a high level of success worked extremely hard to get there. Instead, White privilege should be viewed as a built-in advantage, separate from one's level of income or effort."

Collins goes on to speak about the areas White privilege is leveraged:
In normal everyday life – called the Power of Normal where public spaces, goods and other aspects of everyday life cater to one race and other races are reserved into special sections. According to Collins, this helps White people to move through the world with an expectation that their needs be readily met. People of colour move through the world knowing their needs are on the margins.

In getting the benefit of the doubt – Collins describes White privilege as receiving the benefit of the doubt. White people are seen as individuals while Black people and people of colour are often stereotyped to their particular racial identity. Collins notes that "This has negative effects for people of colour, who, without this privilege, face the consequences of racial profiling, stereotypes and lack of compassion for their struggles."

In accruing accumulated power – Finally Collins speaks about the accumulated power. In her 1988 paper, Peggy McIntosh asked of herself "On a daily basis, what do I have that I didn't earn?" Collins challenges us to answer two follow-up questions:

1. Who built that system and
2. Who keeps it going

This is the root of systemic racism!

You say you envy the Black man for the benefits he may receive; historically speaking that attitude shows you're quite naïve

Have you ever stopped to ask yourself, how he was put in such a position? It's not just because of his life choices or those bad decisions

It's because historically he has been downtrodden and colonized; an entire race of people demeaned, beaten and brutalized

A world built on the superiority of one race over others; using terror, politics and religion, separating children from their mothers

Just because some people of colour appear to be successful; you believe that all is well, and everyone should be thankful

But I guarantee they have all faced the spectre of systemic racism; so, in truth they have succeeded in spite of the system

\*\*\*

## Oh Canada – Part Four

Colonialization is deeply embedded in White supremacy. The horrors visited upon First Nations, Indigenous and Metis peoples in Canada is overpowering testimony to that. Stolen land; broken treaties; destroyed families and residential schools are but a few of the atrocities.

Canada must come to terms with the fact that White supremacy has been – and continues to be – a part of the fabric of its culture. This is the first step in addressing systemic racism.

I mourn at the graves of the children
Innocence lost
Families crushed
Potential unfulfilled
Voices no longer heard
Songs unsung
Spaces left unfilled

\*\*\*

# Enslaved

Language changes over time and BIPOC peoples have been instrumental in ensuring they are properly represented in those changes. An example is the word "slave." Once used to describe the enslaved African, it conjured images of subservient peoples offering little or no resistance to their circumstance.

The dictionary describes a slave as a person who is the property of another person and whose labour and also whose life often is subject to the owner's volition. One who has lost the power of resistance; one who surrenders to something. This was not the enslaved. They fought! They resisted. Their freedom was stripped and stolen but they did not give up.

Who was the real slave?
Thirsting and hungering after greed and power
Selling your soul to the devilish devourer
Sure, you enslaved me against my will
But whose soul was sold to the devil

## Hidden in Plain Sight

Who was the real slave?
Captive junkie to control and domination
Subjugated by your own discrimination
Adamantly refusing to see the disgrace
Of hating another because of their race

Who was the real slave?
Trying to follow the colonial tradition
Willing to use politics and religion
How is it you do not see the facade
To justify enslavement, you even used your God

Who was the real slave?
It was not my people for we were enslaved
We fought and resisted, often right to the grave
Resisting in every way that we could
Fought, so our children's freedom was secured

\*\*\*

# The Mirror

When people think of racism, the spectre of White supremacy generally raises its head. Historically racism has been the marginalization and oppression of people of colour by White people. However, racism or the belief that one race is superior to another, is not the sole domain of White people. We may all have racist or discriminatory attitudes towards people and the belief that only White people can be racist is incorrect.

That being said, historically White people have been the greatest perpetrators of racism against people of colour and that in itself cannot be ignored. What we cannot and should not do is look only to demonize White people in this respect. We must challenge all racism – the racism that we see in our society and the racism that we see in ourselves.

I look ashamedly into the mirror,
horrified at what I see
My own racist attitude smugly staring back at me
Verbal jabs at "Chinese drivers"
Smug remarks about that "Native Indian"
Jokes about "diaper-head" cabbies

All just comes with too much ease

Racism is not just White on Black

it's about supremacy

A contorted twisted illusion in racial hegemony

We all must face the mirror if humanity is to survive

Confront our racist attitudes and set them all aside

Our future is not in racial

or ethnic division

We've tried that many times and failed

For us to improve

humanity's condition, unity must prevail

I pray you to look into the mirror, no matter what your race

That's the first step in our journey to make this world a better place

\*\*\*

## Destroyed

How is it possible to continuously suppress and devastate an entire race of people? First start by treating them as less than human - belittle, demean and subjugate them. Do that for several generations. Teach your children about their superiority. Teach their children about their inferiority. Even when they're eventually granted their "freedom" they are still unable to truly fit in because the society they are freed into was never made for them. Nothing in that society, no single part of that culture was made to build them up.

Even when some seem to be successful, they wrestle with the knowledge that no matter what their financial worth, their skin colour could betray them at any time. For the systems they work and live in were not made to build them up. It was designed to demean, belittle and subjugate them.

My siblings? Purposefully set up to be interrupted and destroyed!
My rightful family taken again and again leaving an aching painful void!
Hearts ripped open again and again with every Trayvon,

Breanna,
Regis,
Sandra Bland,
MLK, and untold others dying like George Floyd!
Secretly raping or openly hunting us like animals; chained, branded, choked, and mercilessly whipped!
Widespread assault of runaway slaves committed as they saw fit
Our physical bodies were literally looted for the taker's monetary use!
While on auction blocks, or even free; subject to severe racial abuse
Not free to cross borders, considered 'on the run', or 'on the loose'
Black males were thrown in jails but more likely hung from the noose
Were Colonizers hearts and minds removed to normalize this depravity?
No. But they bent religion and education into hatred of Blacks: an undiagnosed insanity
Who imagined destroying innocent little children at church on Sunday?
Those of African-descent are still held below contempt and labeled both inferior, as well as uppity!
Dismissed without any restitution because not seeing racism sounds like a handy solution!

We're still invisible service workers; still oppressed; not enough pay to escape poverty!
Me, I get decent pay, still get security guards determined to arrest me at the border, and the TTC!
If I jumped ship, I could've been floating free at the bottom of the sea
But I'm being auctioned off about to be bought as a kitchen commodity

\*\*\*

## I don't mean to be racist, but

There is a Twitter account @YesYoureRacist with the description "If you have to start a sentence with "I'm not racist, but..." then chances are you're pretty racist." BIPOC people know exactly what this feels like. Challenging systemic racism is also challenging someone trying to portray themselves as racially sensitive while spewing racist dialogue

I don't mean to be racist, but...
Seven words beginning a sentence that
Almost always is

Racist...I mean

When taken in context you realize
The speaker knew they were

Racist...I mean

If you knew it was racist and you did not stop
Why should I not think you are

Racist...I mean

Instead, just say it, don't be dismayed
We will know what you are by your words

Racist...I mean

***

## I'm not racist, I have Black friends

Why do People of Colour react negatively whenever they hear the words "I'm not racist, I have [*Insert BIPOC race here*] friends?" This is a symptom of systemic racism. It is so interwoven into the fabric of our society that often people lose sight of the fact that acceptance of a person's remarks by one member of a minority population or oppressed group – does not necessarily mean acceptance by everyone in that group. In fact, there is no Official Seal of Approval for each race, minority or oppressed group that gives someone carte blanche to say whatever they feel without consequence.

In other words – if it sounds racist then it probably is racist! Furthermore, no amount of association with the race, minority population or oppressed group stops it from being racist.

Hey, don't say I'm racist
I have Black friends
They like me
And I like them
We get along so really well
I can't be racist

You can tell
That gives the ability
To speak
With impunity
Because I have
Racial immunity
Nothing I say
Can be offensive
There's no reason
To be defensive
I have Black friends
I am not racist
That's the truth
So, let's embrace it

*\*\**

## I'm not racist, I have White friends

Is reverse racism[xxiii] an insidious myth perpetuated by White supremacy? It's a conversation we must have.

Is reverse racism a thing?
Or
Did you just try to appropriate racism?
Are you really disadvantaged because of your colour?
Or
Oppressed
Marginalized
Disenfranchised
Ever had to fight for equality
For justice in a place that doesn't tolerate diversity
Anyone of you ever been lynched because of your colour?
Did you really just try to appropriate racism?
And play
The victim?

\*\*\*

## I don't understand – A question

Many people point to successful BIPOC peoples as an indicator that racism no longer exists. Just speaking about racism can get some people defensive and argumentative. In many ways this is understandable. But it is not acceptable.

I don't understand why you're complaining so much
You people should just move on
You're acting as if your life is so tough
But I feel that's just simply a con

Slavery is over and done, please just get over it
Damn it man, we're in the twenty-first century
Just stop misbehaving and throwing a fit
Because some White person did not treat you deferentially

Look, here people you have it really good
Some of you are actually doing quite well
Working great jobs, living in nice White neighbourhoods
So why in God's name are you raising hell

What about the Black president, Barack Obama
In a racist country that would never occur
So why the hell are you complaining about trauma
Seems like you're less than sincere

***

Brian Sankarsingh

## Let me explain – The answer

With the context of racism, the undeniable fact is that White people were never enslaved. They were never colonized. They were never forced into segregation. Later on, they never faced real estate covenants that forced them to live in downtrodden ghettos. They did not have to deal with systemized police brutality. There never dealt with job discrimination because of the colour of their skin, and they never faced all these things for countless generations!

You have got to be kidding with all you just said
Can one person really be so badly misinformed
This realization fills me with dread
Makes me feel humanity is damned

I think that you have to get over the fact
That enslaved people were emancipated
It seems you're quite upset by how you act
Because you seem quite frustrated

You're right about the time that we live in
But let me tell you something my friend
All I ask is that you treat me as a human
What we need is equality in the end

Just because a few of us are doing well
Or because we live in nice homes
Doesn't mean the playing field is now equal
Let's stop trying to throw that stone

A White person saying racism is over and done
Really that doesn't make any sense
This is the ignorance we must confront
If we're ever to get over this fence

Let's see what happened after Barack Obama
Donald Trump came into power
Bringing with him White racist nirvana
Those are the type of people he empowered

White people complain about generational trauma
But they don't like to apply it to Blacks
This is not about superficial melodrama
We have always been subject to your attacks

\*\*\*

## Trump card

The name of the 44th President of the United States has become synonymous with many things. Included in this list would be his relentless attitude of divisive and racist rhetoric[xxiv]. When powerful world leaders, through irresponsible words and actions, normalize racist attitudes and verbiage, their supporters are empowered to do the same. Consequently, the entire world suffers.

They were elated when he came down the escalator that day
For what's on their minds, they found someone to say
He used phrases and terms they dare not utter
It was their champion Goliath from down in the gutter
The prejudicial snake that many believe to be dead
He spoke life to it and once again it raised its ugly head
Racial slurs, nicknames, it really didn't matter
He insulted every race that was not of his colour
Opening the flood gates of indifference, he left it ajar
Hate rose from the cracks and crevices near and far
Half-truths and innuendos were his preferred style of speech
There was no law in his mind he wasn't willing to breech
He told them he can make it great again

## Hidden in Plain Sight

They loaded their weapons for a country to defend
Names of hate groups some unknown and some presumed dead
Proudly assumed their positions to evoke a sense of dread
The sheets and hoods may no longer be worn
But the heart bleeds the same from the bite of the tongue
Though the evil they feared were in their imagination
The real threat was now heading for inauguration
Who would have thought that evangelicals with bible in hand
Would praise and adore such a vile man
After blatantly admitting to have women's privates in his clutch
One would think they'd say "No that's too much"
Many prayed for the nightmare to come to an end
Those that profited around him had to pretend
Muslims were banned and Mexicans walled out
The unconcealed discrimination was beyond a shadow of a doubt
Allies who were once loyal hung their heads in shame
To be seen in his company, some just played the game
The bigoted rejoiced for their messiah's coming was stark
But it was the beast who their foreheads did mark
Just as we were beginning to think, he now has to go
He hatched a devious plan for a hostile overthrow
A similar Black gathering would've been dispersed

With their White counterpart it was certainly the reverse
With Jim trying to sound like a young rooster learning to crow
Make it clear to that old fowl cock, on that journey we're not willing to go
Those magic beans of racism they got wet and grew in this land
Though the tree has been hewn, the roots are buried deep in the sand
And from time to time another charlatan will allow a branch to grow
But we'll let the axe of our voices strike yet another blow

Though race is a social construct, matters such as
Shadeism, debates about Black-on-Black crime, continues

\*\*\*

## The Mad King

BIPOC peoples were giddy with elation when a Black man rose to the office of the President of the United States[xxv]. Many felt that they were living MLK Jr's. dream[xxvi]. But what happened? How did the country go from a Black President to a President who openly supported White supremacy[xxvii]? Most importantly why?

The mad king proudly refused to leave
Knowing there'd eventually be no reprieve
Instead, he blatantly solicited his support
To be ready for a civil war

So many tantrums, our proud king did throw
While democracy suffered from his many blows
But thankfully that ship has finally sailed
As his bid to continue ruling eventually failed

He dreamed of being king and master forever
But the people pronounced "no not ever!"
What a great spectacle was that revolt
To see the king's grab for power revoked

The moral of the story I'll tell you my friend
At no time should you ever solely depend
On dividing the people in order to rule
Or be ceremoniously, cast out as the fool

***

# 1 - Go back to your own country

This is one of the most common statements made by White people to BIPOC peoples. It is steeped in ignorance and racism and reeks of colonial entitlement. What's unfortunate, is that it has been heard by BIPOC peoples all over the world. It's the 'go-to' racist response.

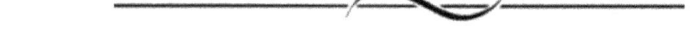

Go back to your own country
You're only here to complain
It's quite elementary
Doesn't take much of a brain

You people like our way of life
But you don't want to work
This is the epitome
Of you disgusting immigrant jerks

\*\*\*

## 2 - No! You go back first

What some people conveniently tend to forget is that unless you are Indigenous, First Nations or Metis then you are a settler. No one else can claim to be to be native to Canada. We are all settlers! Let that sink in. No matter how many "generations" of yours have been in Canada, you are a settler. No matter if you just got your Canadian citizenship, you are a settler.

I'll leave when you leave
Because this is not your native land
You stole it from someone else
You have no right to issue commands

First you say we don't want to work
Then we're here to steal your jobs
Make up your mind it's not that hard
To recover from this faux pas

\*\*\*

## Oh Canada – Part Five

People often speak about going back to times when life was simple. That means different things to different people. What is a White person thinking about when they dream of a 'simpler' time? What would a First Nations, Indigenous or Metis person think about as "simpler times?"

Understanding the systems that were put in place to create Canada is another way of understanding systemic racism.

My word was enough for my people
It belonged to me
I to it
But the White man came with his writing
And said my word was not
Good anymore
He said there was something
Even better
Than my pledge
That I've never broken!

Sign a treaty on paper, it
Would stand the test of
Father Time
I had to put my thumb print
To paper
Which made me wonder if
I ever lose that finger
How would they know
It was me

My word has proven to be much
Stronger
Than the lies that we were told
On that paper

***

## A Legacy of Hate

We must all challenge hate and White supremacy. Nevertheless, while having conversations about how to heal our BIPOC communities and how to address discrimination and systemic racism are important conversations – they must keep space for our allies.

What do you hear when a person says
"I can't breathe?"
What do these words convey
Was it only George Floyd's neck that a knee was on
Or was it ours as well
What do you see when I wear a hoodie
What does that mean to you
Do you first need to see the colour of my skin
Before making a life and death decision
Forced to live in ghettos
Surround by abject poverty
Neighbourhoods overrun with violent crime
Forced to depend on a system
That was meant to oppress
These things were not our choice
But we stand in blame for them
Yet you scream reverse racism

Whenever we demand equality
When we ask for justice
Or demand systemic change
Unwilling to let go of a seedy past
Grasping tightly at racist memories
Reluctant to change xenophobic language
Averse to seeing other races excel
Stuck in the shadows of your White supremacy
You pass on this hate as your own legacy

***

## Being Brown

Though race is a social construct, matters such as Shadeism, debates about Black-on-Black crime, continuous societal pressures and instances of violence targeting BIPOC peoples often lead them to hate the very skin they're in.

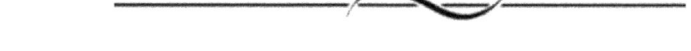

I hate the colour of my skin
With an abiding hate that
I cannot seem to overcome
Is this quote, unquote
Abnormal?

Does it sound too cliché?
Do any other Brown people feel this way?
Lost in a deep, dark, destitute place,
Embarrassed and forlorn

Wondering could I ever be
Normal?
This fills me with dismay?
Have you ever felt this way?

Try as I might, I am eluded in
My quest to find a reason
For being born this colour
Is it useless for me to try and be
Normal?
Every day is Judgement Day
My skin colour has betrayed me

***

## A White perspective

This poem was written by one of our White poets as she sat in a hospital waiting room. It is poignant and agonizing just in the question it asks. Unfortunately, statistics[xxviii] show that many BIPOC peoples are not treated equally even here.

As I sit in a hospital, anticipating
I see many others sitting and waiting
Men, women, of many different races
Do others get treated differently depending on their faces?

This is one place where everyone
Appears to be treated the same
Which is how life should be everywhere
No matter your worth or fame

\*\*\*

## Doctor Racist

Many studies[xxix] have showed that racial bias exists in medicine; however, beyond that there are many stories in the United States and Canada of this racial bias. This should not be construed as disparagement to all medical professionals as indeed there are many who are only concerned with the health and wellbeing of all the people under their care. What this shows, however, is that even in medicine, systemic racism exists.

I respect my Hippocratic Oath[xxx]
It's the cornerstone of my profession
My dedication to that Oath evokes
My clinical designation

I have sworn to do no harm
Neither shall I do injustice
My care shall be shelter from the storm
Respect the lives to which I am entrusted

Don't ask me how I know that young Black man[xxxi]
Is only here seeking free drugs
I assure he is in no real pain
I am wise to his tricks and shams

I read somewhere that science proved
Black women have greater pain tolerance[xxxii]
Or maybe that's just something I assumed
Quite simply a racial aberrance

***

## Judge Racist

There is no doubt that racism against BIPOC peoples has been present in the Justice system in both Canada[xxxiii] and the United States. This is just one more example of systemic racism at the institutional level. Like all types of systemic racism, it too has the power to negatively affect lives and families.

Justice is blind or so they say
But sometimes she sees skin colour
The darker the skin, so says the survey
The sentence will be much tougher

Black, Indigenous, Person of Colour[xxxiv]
Chances are you'll be detained
Get yourself ready, say goodbye to your mother
So the status quo can be maintained

But if you're White, you might be too pretty for jail[xxxv]
For sure your sentence will be minimal
One has to wonder about Lady Justice's scale
They're in your favour if you're a White criminal

\*\*\*

## Officer Racist

Systemic racism exists in policing, exists both in Canada[xxxvi] and the United States[xxxvii]. Communities of colour have felt the violence of policing from the time of enslavement, through to segregation and today. This brutality and bloodshed is more often than not aimed squarely between the shoulders of Black boys and men, leaving a trail of broken lives in its wake.

Decades of blood stains your hands
Flowing from the past into tomorrow
It seems like a characteristic of your brand
Bringing death and sorrow

You say you're here to serve and protect
But what about communities of colour
They never get the same respect
Seems you try to make them suffer

So where do we go from here
You hear us crying "defund the police"
We don't say that out of fear
It's because we simply want peace

You're no longer hunting runaways
Escaping from the plantation
We've long gone past enslavement days
While you're still in violent stagnation

It's not one bad apple in the bunch
This hate is institutional
You can no longer use that crutch
It makes you appear criminal

Your job is about community
Especially helping those of colour
It's not about violence and brutality
It's about helping one another

***

## Born a Racist

Are people born racist? Or is it learned?

Will there ever be a time when we don't see between White and Black
A time when a person's colour is enough to set them back?
Forever fighting for the right to be seen as a human being?
When can Black men go about their lives without risking a beating?
Will Lady Justice ever truly be blind to the colour of my skin?
When I will be considered for the man I am and not my melanin?
Will there ever come a time, when we all live in harmony?
When either race, colour or ethnicity is not the cause of some controversy?
When will people finally accept systemic racism is real?
That for Black people and people of colour it's an everyday ordeal?
Martin Luther King Jr. had a dream in nineteen sixty-three
And in that dream, every single human being was truly free
We fought for desegregation and then for our civil rights
Brilliant men like MLK Jr. and Malcolm X paid the price
We have to fight at every turn, while you live larger than life

Meanwhile law enforcement makes even our colour a crime
Our Black men are incarcerated, stolen from their families
Our children brought up in broken homes, the ultimate casualty
When will you ever see, we've been losing from the start
These systems were setup to oppress us and to rip our lives apart
Please open your eyes and realise, we still need your support
No person is born a racist my friend, that kind of hate is taught

***

## Micro Aggression

Microaggression is described as any interaction between those of different races, culture or genders that can be interpreted as non-physical aggression. Many BIPOC peoples must struggle daily with microaggression which, in its own insidious way is a part of systemic racism.

What's the size of a pin-prick and as destructive as a mac truck
Causing damage to your insides, your psyche and all your stuff?
Lately it's called a 'micro-aggression'
The injuries to our existence are equal in measure
Appearing in normalized conversations these attacks on BIPOC reputations quickly draw blood with no provocation
Some White-privileged people tend to think it's all their space
And knock loudly on the window of my own place
To ask me: "What are you doing in there?"
For the privileged 'telling it like it is' often comes into play, except they rarely play fair
especially if I'm not somewhere
where they expect/prefer I should be

This is how many BIPOC exist within the wider community
Sustaining serious emotional harm that seems to float in the air
We're pushed right into it daily and there are no protections
from these mind-games recently called 'micro-aggressions.
"I know that's not what your real hair is like." "You can't be the Manager here." This food's too spicy but I'm sure you'll like it." "This is so well-written, I'm sure you didn't write it"
"Btw I like it better when you wear your hair the other way."
"I'm sure you'll let me in line first, since I have to get back to my important work!"
In the stores they follow BIPOC with their eyes
Staff are trained to automatically criminalize
and if you ask to try a garment on for size
they say. "O.K. But bring it right... back... here.
Sparking so much hurt and the very anger they fear

Recipients of these invisible snippets of hate in disguise
slowly die on the inside as we're expected to take it and smile
at superior-feeling folks who know they're protected in society

while playing a part to ensure BIPOC feel rejection and anxiety

So many "good upper-class people" claim to be race tolerant
With never an off-colour word, and no racial rants heard (?)
plus, they would never even think to utter a racial slur
"After all, a person of colour is married to my brother"
...Yet with pure impunity their children repeat "Daniel Boone was a man" ... and other mean racist rhymes
since they learned like all national past-times there are social rewards
Kids get off the hook for using words out of the muck of ages
"Oh, come on now, you can't really believe my kids are racist!"
"They didn't use the n-word, they were just tryna say negro"
Not too harshly corrected for copying the adults in their world who failed to be as tolerant or polite about the different races when stressed out at home with the family behind closed doors
Why not jump on the biased bandwagon, eh?
Racial lies are broadcast on TV screens all day!
A smear campaign is what we're dealing with daily

Stereotyping the lives of all people of African descent
The racist campaign knows nothing, but says a helluvalot
Making racial narratives appear as truth, but they're not!

During problematic public displays of racial hatred
There is rarely any warning, and nothing is sacred!
Passed off as simple misunderstandings or harmless jokes
Or just "innocent" statements popping up unprovoked
Is it your fault someone is so sensitive and feels choked?

On an otherwise beautiful day in the neighborhood
Racial barbs and race-baiting interrupt everything good
Right after they happen there's, like, no tangible proof
Except our collective blood pressure rises through the roof!
These incidents are brief, but not micro, not tiny l'il lessons
Call it what it truly is: heartless racial aggression

***

## Shades

Shadeism is prejudice based on skin tone. More than usually, the preference is for lighter-skinned people. I have seen this in my own family, where a darker child is given less attention than their fairer sibling. Shadesim literally puts White supremacy in the shade. We talk about black being beautiful yet the market for skin lightening products is in the billions.[xxxviii]

We need to change the narrative. Shadeism is a type of White supremacy, and it is destroying our communities of colour.

White says there are no shades
If you're not White, you're Black
White demands there be no Gray
This truth must remain intact

But White has no reservation
About pitting Black against Brown
Seeking only its supreme preservation
In their colourful meltdown

So Black and Brown struggle
To impress their White enslavers
White stands by and chuckles
At their colourful disaster

Black and Brown don't realize
They're being played for a fool
The purpose of White's reason lies
In the idiom, "divide and rule"

They continue to fight each other
While White rules unrestrained
Brother fighting brother
Until no colour remains

What makes this so much harder
Is that Shades of Black and Brown
Take up arms against each other
In a Shadeism showdown

As a person of colour
I mourn this senseless fight
Black and Brown are both my brothers
To survive we must unite

\*\*\*

## Black Lives Matter Too

A White person responding to the words Black Lives Matter with All Lives Matter is like them saying systemic racism does not exist. Of course, it does not exist – for them. The All Lives Matter response may sound inclusive, but it is intended to shut down conversation. It ignores history. It overlooks and discounts the daily realities of BIPOC peoples. It minimizes their lived experiences.

When you respond "All lives matter"
Do you believe we doubt that to be true
If we do, have you ever asked yourself
Why do we say Black Lives Matter <u>too</u>

\*\*\*

# 1ne Race

Like Martin Luther King Jr. BIPOC people still dream of a better world. One filled with acceptance, unity and love. We know it's possible. We have seen people change; but not fast enough. BIPOC peoples are consistently asked to wait – to exercise patience; but the time for waiting is too far gone. We now demand! We protest! We shout! Change must happen now!

We know how deeply racism is embedded in all systems now
Wouldn't it be exciting to change the reality of our world right now?
Forget the strife, unite and unlearn it all somehow?
What a relief it would be to agree, and for our children to abolish all these bloody endless wars
Put together caring policies where there've been none before unless it was only lip service or merely in written reports
but not followed up with positive action to stop the hurt
Imagine employing real peacekeepers who don't carry guns or any weapons at all
No punishing, but compassionate help; equity and status for all

Let's have a mandate for fair sharing of our economic wealth
No need to use and abuse service workers and risk their health.
In fact, no slaves or servants at all and no human trafficking;
No pipelines; No plunder of Indigenous land; and No fracking! No court injunctions; No more deportations; No immigration detention centres as we know they are jails without any access to get bail or mail, or legal representation
No more hoarding, No more extractive capitalism;
No car-towing schemes, No racial profiling; No TTC fines; Stop property owners from seeing people only as dollar signs;
No more real estate magnates running rampant over our right to have homes, or even just affordable housing.
No gun manufacturing companies; No contract-flipping and no more gig-job schemes where bosses have no accountability
No more pulling the rug out from under migrants' dreams

But first get Indigenous fishers more licences; honor treaties; and bring clean water into every single one of their neglected communities

If North America does not do this, and Indigenous rights remain dismissed then what are our chances of everyone being free?
Because if only some of us are, then none of us can be.
This is the entire equation underlying the true meaning of truth, reconciliation, and accountability

Together all of us can learn to unite in the future. But how?
If we finally follow leadership to stop all racial tensions now

The best way to survive on this planet is with ancient African and Indigenous proven wisdom throughout the ages;
And the best way to thrive on this planet is for all races to stop human trafficking and stop voting in political leaders who are capitalist patriarchal colonial racists

Surviving united means not endorsing separate political teams
Everyone's dreams of local and international peace means
Working united for the good of all human beings in all nations
Recognize human dignity and the need for self-determination

Abolish racism to humanize and recognize one human race

Who's with me on this journey to a peaceful change of pace? Transforming all the hateful messages, too, would be so great since humans need more love and hope and lots less hate

***

## Jameila's Reflections

Ever since she was a child, Jameila Alford felt a connection with her ancestors. Although she did not know of Mufa or Tattio their spirit of resistance and commitment to freedom resonated in every part of her being. The verse that was so important to Mufa was his greatest legacy.

That verse reminded Mufa of his home and his identity even when he was faced with the harsh reality of enslavement. Passing it down the generations, it became a lighthouse guiding his descendants. Showing them that their identity was not only about where they were from. It was about who they chose to be – through the direst of circumstances. She was indeed a child of the Kingdom of Nri.

My dearest ancestor, whoever you are
I wonder how you felt when you were abducted
Brought unwillingly to these shores
A life once free and then restricted

## Hidden in Plain Sight

I sometimes dream of placing my hand in yours
Hear myself telling you one day we will be free
Hold on dear one, you must endure
It is my guarantee

I think of my ancestor who was so hasty
To help a White woman when she tripped
Having no second thought for his own safety
A kindness that would get him killed

But for the pain you all had to bear
They tried to shame you for the colour of your skin
You never wavered, never despaired
Never felt chagrined

Now as I approach the end of my own life
I hope I've made you proud
Each one of you have been my guide
Keeping me away from doubt

By my example, I've showed what we can achieve
I have passed on the importance of unity
I pray that all others will come to know and believe
The strength, power and talent in our community

For I am a child of the Kingdom of Nri
I believe all men are born to be free
This gift was granted by Chukwu to all
That enter into Nri's great hall

***

## ...for my young brother, Tony

This deeply personal poem was written to show the terrible disparity, racism and hate that actually existed in Canada. This poem stands as a stark reminder of the pain and suffering experienced by many of our fellow Black Canadians.

I was born in May of 1959; my l'il bro was born in June of 1961
I don't recall really; we met briefly in a foster home; I was 3 and he was 1
He was sent to another foster home, while I stayed in the same place
I always knew this part, and was told the rules were 'never try to trace'
Any familial connection we may have had was already cleanly erased
"You're adopted over here on this side of town; he's adopted over there
No need to worry or wonder further because you're both in good care" Right?
Fast forward 50 yrs: The Universe sends some unusual news by phone

It's kind of a strange story already and one I thought I'd already 'known'

The call is from past schoolmate Monique who I'd not seen since Gr.4

Her foster mom sick in hospital told a secret she couldn't keep anymore

"Your old schoolmate, Laurie, is the bio sis of your foster bro from yrs. ago!"

Monique's mind is blown, and she gets busy tracking me down by phone

So, she passed that info to me and I said I already knew I had a brother

But that was all I knew; we'd never met except for briefly when toddlers

She said she not only met Tony, but he was her long-lost foster brother!

But hasn't seen him since he was 17 when she got married at almost 20, he told her, he was leaving Canada and moving to Florida to try to make some money

**Young Tony**

L'il Tony was forced to attend French school on the other side of the bridge

No one ever knew why. No one gives answers like this to foster kids

Few Black people lived here in the '60s; so much hardship was added to the mix
No one spoke French in the foster home; Tony must've had a hard time of it.

### Young Laurie and Monique

She'd invited me to play at recess; I was the only Black kid in the school
'65 -'69 Monique and I were bff's until I was 10 and sent to a different school
She never said she had a Blk bro at home making it easy to choose me
I didn't know she was a foster child at all, also at the same time as me!
It didn't come up between li'l kids busy playing and learning how to read!

Back to the strange significance of Tony and me
As were both being fostered in status quo secrecy
but with our foster homes in pretty much the same vicinity
which I guess would make secrecy an even higher priority
Handled adeptly by child welfare, backed up by school authority
Such a big problem if we ever bumped into each other? Why?

In sending young Tony off to French school on the far side of town
Although he lived in a foster home very near to the English school I attended, and was also beside the church I was always around
The co-op of 2 sets of foster parents had to be tight for this to go down
So now it's clear that this entire small town church community
agreed it would be 'safer' for two Black siblings to never meet
We'll never know the real reasons for such secrecy, will we?
Unless it's confessed as their best way to break apart families

But just think of the strange manipulations that had to abound
In sending young Tony to French school on the far side of town
If child welfare orchestrated it all, is their job protection or deception?
A number of arbitrary rules in T&M[3]'s' home was never questioned

---

[3] Tony and Monique

Any foster parent, or adoptive ones, knew every rule and toed every line
Especially mine…God bless their souls; they went to heaven in 2011
Neither breathed a word to me; never broke the rules the entire time.
I'd know nothing of this if T&M's old foster mom hadn't thought it wise to break deceptive rules of secrecy and expose truth before her demise;
In her heart realizing child welfare secrecy only helps to destroy lives

***

# Tired

"Get over it, racism is in the past and now in the 21st century we should be over it. The USA had a Black man serve in the Office of the President for crying out loud!"

Is racism over?
Was having a Black man as President of the United States the measurement that it was over?

It borders on irony when White people tell Black people and People of colour that they should move on because racism is in the past. Just as they are tired hearing about it BIPOC people are tired of experiencing it.

You complain that you are tired
Of hearing about racism
This kind of talk should be retired
Our society has evolved

Why should we keep holding
Racism up to your face
You claim that it's depressing
It was a past disgrace

## Hidden in Plain Sight

Come on now, get over it
That's all in the past
Put it into a dark closet
And let it breathe its last

Interesting that you would say
We stop talking about racial hate
In many ways your words betray
A desperate need to obfuscate

It gives me so satisfaction
But I have a few questions for you
Your response will be a demonstration
Of whether what you seek is the truth

How can you know racism is ended
How can you appreciate my plight
You who have never been affected
Because your colour is White

\*\*\*

## The Reality of our Lives

We often say that history ignored is bound to be repeated, however history itself has proven that whether it is ignored or not, it will repeat. The brutality of the First World War, was the impetus of the creation of the League of Nations. "Never again!" was the motto on everyone's lips. In two decades, the world was back at it. All the lessons learned were forgotten, all the promises and treaties ignored. What implications does this have for thorny an issue like racism?

You can't take it with you is the popular refrain
Yet most of us spend our lives riding that train
Accumulating wealth and possessions aplenty
While hearts and souls lay barren and empty
But what is it worth…our frail human life
We are but a spark in a universe of light
Shining so bright for what amounts to an instant
Then to burn out, disappear from existence
Are we the sum of our fears or our follies
Or just biological matter encased in bodies
We ask what's the reason for our existence
A celestial purpose, or measly subsistence
Should it be about owning possessions

Or is it being blindly immersed in religion
Both of these paths end in a type of destruction
Each has their own peculiar sinful seduction
With such a dismal outlook on reality
What does our life mean in actuality
If left unchecked man will ruin all things
That is his way, be he pauper or king
History has proven it time and again
And much of humanity has suffered the pain
Millions sacrificed in conflict and wars
We're told power vacuums is what nature abhors
The lives of the young are bartered for the old
All in a desperate bid for control
Countless people are dying from disease and starvation
While we choose to spend millions on one man's coronation
Lives being taken in brutal random shootings
Dodging a bullet is now part of their schooling
And when reality is manifested in their fears
All that is offered is useless thoughts and prayers
This world is a mess and there is no denying
Whatever's being sold, I don't feel like buying
The wealthy tell the poor "Being rich is a burden"
But if you're too poor to eat, how can that be for certain
They say that the struggle is what makes it worthwhile
Even as they "languish" in opulence and style

Don't turn to religion it's another system of control
They take all your money in exchange for your soul
Or else they abuse you in many other ways
All the while demanding that you give their god praise
Multi-million-dollar churches, but people are suffering
Priests and pastors live grandly while parishioners are struggling
It is quite difficult to reconcile that equation
Without experiencing a certain degree of frustration
Selfishness and avarice require you look after yourself
Steal as much as you can, build your generational wealth
I feel by now dear reader you must be getting depressed
By all the negative statements I have expressed
Seems like the world is going to hell in a handbasket
And our only sure exit is going out in a casket
I do not deny that things surely look bleak
But maybe it's time we turn the other cheek
There will be people who trade in hate and fear
Whose reactions will be violent, fierce and severe
There will always be criminals, thieves and killers
Always be despots, tyrants and wanna-be Hitlers
There will always be those entitled and narcissistic
Those who choose to be wicked and sadistic
This is the reality of what it means to be human
It is a dichotomy and a source of confusion
We are cursed to understand our mortality

But that does not affect everyone's morality
Some see this as an opportunity to be truly selfless
Others use it as an excuse to pretend to be helpless
Still others are driven to be lawgiver and king
Along with the power and control these roles bring
Despite the path you take and how you choose to behave
One thing is assured us and that is the grave
You can't take it with you, but your character matters
That is what will be remembered forever after

\*\*\*

# I don't want to World

Often people just get tired of fighting the same battles and arguing the same points. But, at what point do we simply give up and just say "I no longer wish to participate." Even more importantly, what must we do to make sure people never get to that point?

I've decided I don't want to world anymore
I think I'd much prefer to be left alone
It feels like life is becoming a chore
Stupidity is now humanity's capstone

First, we hated the Christians
For their backwater religion
This was a sin worthy of crucifixion
For anyone under Roman suspicion

Then as time went on we persecuted the Jews
This for the 'new sin' of hating the Christians
Consequently, we heaped on the abuse
Belittle the people and deride their religion

Indigenous tribes did not fare any better
Persecuted and forced into bondage
Many would perish because of the pressure
Serve us or die, was the clear message

## Hidden in Plain Sight

Yes, I'm sure I don't want to world anymore
It feels like we're a disease without a cure

Those same "Christians" who were once hated
Now used their religion to rule mankind
And for the rest of time, it will be hotly debated
Is this what Christ wanted, was this his design?

Black, Brown and any other person of colour
Now faced the whip of the colonial master
If you were not white you were seen as the "other"
Now came the time of celebrating alabaster

We survived segregation, but not without schisms
Brother fighting brother for racial equality
Soon we would talk about evil communism
In hating the "other" we find camaraderie

Pretty sure I just don't want to world from today
It's getting too much, something must give way

We've killed millions of people, in hundreds of wars
Oppressed and tormented innocent souls
Even animals haven't escaped our ravenous jaws
In our fleeting attempts at greed and control

One man wants to lord his power over another
Caring little for the pain and anguish it brings
A level of depravity not limited by colour
Some people are just driven to do evil things

Growing older has taught me one simple truth
Money is not the root of all evil
The hate that we harbour is learned in our youth
It's something within us, something gross and primeval

Some are driven by greed, hate, lust and revenge
Some just want ruin and destruction
Others don't care who they hurt or offend
They stop at nothing to fuel their addiction

I'm starting to think I don't want to world
For all that I've read, heard and observed

The pain and misery of others give some people joy
They revel when others feel pain
They're happy to see the lives of others destroyed
In their eyes peace and love are profane

Is it possible to solve this riddle of hate?
Can we ever hope for peace in our time?
Some say that we can, if we simply have faith
The answer they profess is in the divine

But is it a cop out, waiting on divine intervention
While violence is committed in a divine name
Sins easily forgiven with complete abrogation
A horrific part of a twisted divine game

Meanwhile widows and orphans, the poor and downtrodden
Suffer from pious men and their evil ways
The more I experience it the more that I know
I am pretty sure, I just don't want to world

***

# Duality

Human beings find comfort in categorizing, classifying and cataloguing the world they live in. This has been our greatest strength and or most horrible weakness because when we start to categorize ourselves we begin to make unnecessary judgments on people that may not look and act like us.

Heaven, Hell
Are these, two sides of the same coin?
Good, Bad
Happy, Sad
One seems so much easier to malign

Us against Them
Beat down the Stranger
They don't look like us
They must be a danger

Black against White
Please beat them down
And let's not forget about
Yellow and Brown

My views are right
My god is much stronger
He will win in the end for
He is the conqueror

I know what's best for
All of humanity
I have all the answers and
All else is profanity

Hot, Cold
Weak, Bold
Surely the coin can be turned over
Dirty, Clean
Outside, In
Let's all try to find the impostor
I must play the victim
Then I will be the heel
When will this ever end?
This vicious double deal

Rich against Poor
A historical misalignment
One above the other
In perpetual disagreement

War, Peace
Predictable, Caprice
Always we stand against one another
Enemy, Friend
Beginning, End
But what happens if the other is your brother

***

## 1 - My Brothers, White

These final three poems were intentionally placed at the end of this book. They are a call to action; challenging us all to be and do better. Each poem in this book, exposed you to the pain, anguish and grief of BIPOC peoples. But we cannot end on such a note.

We want to leave you with that sense of optimism. Not blind baseless optimism – but actionable optimism. BIPOC peoples, by their very nature are optimistic. They look for the good even when confronted with the agony of the bad. We hope, dear reader, that you will join us in our quest for equality as a friend, an ally and a fellow human being.

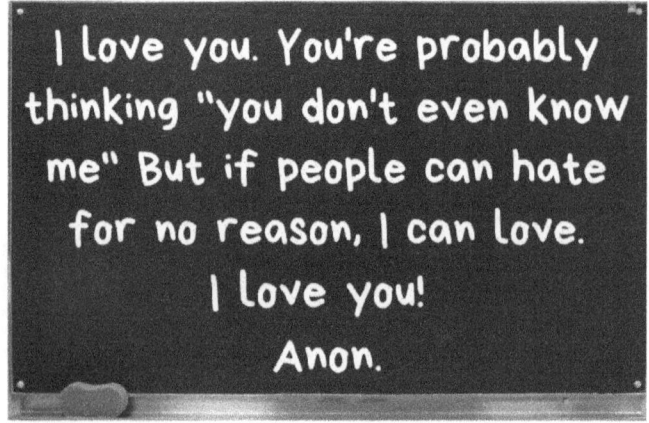

Figure 3 - A quotation by an anonymous source

Brian Sankarsingh

My White brothers I'm speaking to some not all
For your lack of understanding I am appalled
You came across the Atlantic and plundered the native
Contemplating the act, you wrote your own narrative
Standing tall you pretend to be brave
In your desire to get rich, an entire race you enslave
Your quest for superiority knows no bounds
You continue to make claims on baseless grounds
This great land of ours isn't yours nor mine
We all came from somewhere, that's the bottom line

The wrong you've perpetrated, you refuse to acknowledge
Claiming your ancestry affords you White privilege
If we are equal, then why is it so hard
To live in your neighborhood and mow my own yard
If the colour of my skin, you view as a threat
The abuse of my ancestors should bring utter regret
Your harden heart could bleed no remorse
For the identity stolen and taken by force
Study the words of the God you claim to love and praise
Yourself you'll condemn when you consider your ways

Send them back because their colour takes a certain hue
But many were born here just like you

## Hidden in Plain Sight

It's a shame you won't stop playing this stupid game
Forgetting that your parents also came
The blood in our veins, the same RH factor
When donated, it's not labeled by colour
A pint to live, when needed in your case
You'll gladly take, you're not concerned with race
Maybe one day you'd appreciate our plight
And take a bold stand for that which is right

Fake smiles and handshakes your pseudo gesture
To then wash your hands as though touching a leper
The derogatory term for us you seem to prefer
Doesn't make you any more superior
Holding me down and allowing your kind to excel
Would only strengthen my reserve to rebel
Brutal suppression causing our light to flicker
But in the heart of our offspring still glows the ember
You frown at injustice in other parts of the world
Yet practice hatred to peril of your soul

Wake up! It's not coffee you smell but profound arrogance
Eating your insides is the cancer of indifference
Deep in the recesses of you heart is a cure for your blindness
'Twill afford you a life to treat all with kindness
We will continue to dismantle your unholy writ

As to this fight for equality we whole heartedly commit
Those not like you that you hate and detest
Without hesitation will assist in your distress
Be wise my brother and make a wise choice
Let goodness and mercy echo from your voice

***

## 2 - My Brothers, Black

My Black brothers I'm talking to some not all
Your behavior truly has me appalled
Your ancestors were slaves, but you are free
But with freedom comes great responsibility
The slick words you use on the ladies you charm
In your mind you think it causes no harm
Women are not tools that you use at your pleasure
They're God's gift to you, their bodies you should treasure
Many of the eggs you fertilized ends up with a name
Ignoring your duty to support should cause you shame
Growing up for you was hard without a father
Is this the life for your child you would rather?

The brilliant brain you got above your shoulders
Can do much more than just carrying boulders
You too can create, invest, and become great
So stop waiting for crumbs off the boss' plate
Develop a sense of pride about who you are
It should be more than just working to buy a sports car
The songs you sing that promotes violence
Why not write one that inspires excellence
Can you be trusted to be on time on the job
Or are you to hangover from the event at the club
Don't copy the excuse, "because I'm Black"

Rise from the ashes and carve your own track

Gang bangers and drug dealers live like there's no lack
Many end in an early grave where there's no coming back
The way you speak, dress, and your deportment is a factor
It should always tell volumes about your character
Don't intentionally be a part of the racial profile
Then spend the rest of your life living in exile
Create a path that your offspring could gladly follow
Today is yours, you're not sure of tomorrow
Your life is not defined by the oppression you see
You have a part in shaping your destiny
The negativity is there to keep you believing
That nothing you dream is worth achieving

A carefree lifestyle offers little to no reward
Map out your progress and keep moving forward
That repugnant fashion you so ardently wear
Lift your pants up, stop showing people your rear
Wear pride and dignity, and let trustworthiness be your guide
For your various faults it will continuously hide
Respect for others should be your first passage to peace
Your personality should sell you, not list you with the deceased
The money you make should not only be to spend

Let it work for you, invest, strategize and for profit, lend
All that you are is more than what you can fathom
Never settle for the dross at the very bottom

My brother, your attitude leaves much to be desired
Taken too young, is the mantra for some who've expired
A life of crime has a very short future
Much shorter than the post of your illicit behavior
Obscenity and absurdity that you think is a fad
When uploaded on social media, makes the race look bad
A life of revenge is only seen as abhorrent
You're not owed for what was done to your fore parents
Conquer hate with love that knows no reservation
Don't be a catalyst to society's destruction
And when evil assails, and the enemy encroach
Hold you head up high and you name above reproach

***

## Colour Blindness

What is the colour of fury
Destruction in all its glory
Is it burning fiery red
Or black as the night is dead
And what about its opposite
Is there a colour to serenity
A calming blue or verdant green
Or some such colour in between
If fury does claim red as its colour
What colour then, does love favour
Can both emotions claim the same
Or is this a childish parlour game
We've been told a coward's yellow
A colour often used for pleasure
While sadness, guilt and fear are black
Somehow these things seem out of whack
We use colour to associate
Emotions and feelings in aggregate
But colours are used for other things
Such as the colour of your skin
Certain colours can grant entry
While others are seen as unfriendly
Some colours are seen as exclusive
Other colours are quite obtrusive

This has been true for most of history
It's one of our most complicated mysteries
The further back in time we go
The less that colours seem to show
But closer to the present-day
Humanity takes a different pathway
Using colour for segregation
Seems an unholy aberration
How do we turn back the hands of time
To shift this colour paradigm
If we don't our fate is sealed
Traversing the colour minefield
Please don't be so quick to dismiss
Playing games this close to the abyss
If we continue in this trajectory
It will surely be a bitter victory
The colour that wins the colour war
Wins nothing more than blood and gore
Our mutual destruction is assured
Continuing down this desolate road
Though the solution is challenging
It all comes down to dismantling
The colour construct must be dismantled
The whole idea has been mishandled
We go back to the basics
Of our shared humanity, not our genetics

We must all become blind to colour
A thought I know some will think vulgar
It's not easy to dismiss the pain
Or racism that has been ingrained
But someone has to raise the standard
Raise the bar and lead the vanguard
And who better than people of colour
The ones who have been seen as "the other"
Let's start by not trying to demonize
Any others who want to be our allies
Even if we must begin the conversation
It cannot continue without cooperation
That means every person can weigh in
It's the only way humanity wins

Make sure to read,

Enslaved, Chronicle of Resistance Book I
The Lamentation of the Enslaved

And

Enslaved, Chronicle of Resistance Book II
Freedom Bells are Ringing

And

Enslaved, Chronicle of Resistance Book IV
A Companion Reader

# Table of Figures

FIGURE 1 - HIDDEN IN PLAIN SIGHT ...................................................................... 15
FIGURE 2 - MUFA'S FAMILY TREE PT 2 ..................................................................... 1
FIGURE 3 - A QUOTATION BY AN ANONYMOUS SOURCE ............................................. 168

## Biographies and Poems

Brian Sankarsingh

SANKARSINGH is a Trinidadian-born Canadian immigrant who has published several books of poetry on a wide range of social and historical themes including racism, colonialism and enslavement. These topics are intimately intertwined with Sankarsingh's professional work with the Alliance for Healthier Communities. Sankarsingh artfully blends prose and poetry into his storytelling creating an eclectic mix with both genres. This unique approach is sure to provide something for everyone.

His debut book, A Sliver of a Chance, received several 5-star reviews from The Prairies Book Review, BookView Review, Red Headed Book Lover, OnlineBookClub and Readers Favourite.

# Register of poems

## ERA 3
1. I am Jameila Alford
2. Setting the stage
3. Good news…Slavery's Abolished!
4. …No! You're wrong!
5. A dream
6. What will tomorrow bring
7. One Bad Apple
8. Jameila and Grandma Dot
9. Oh Canada – Part I
10. It's not all Black and White
11. Break the Cycle
12. Oh Canada – Part II
13. The Black in BIPOC
14. The Indigenous in BIPOC
15. The People of Colour in BIPOC
16. Oh Canada - Part III
17. Sinful Fraternization
18. Part 1 - Symbols
19. Part 2 - Symbols
20. Hidden In Plain Sight
21. Systemic Change
22. Part 1 – I wish I were Black
23. Part 2 – You have no idea what you're talking about
24. Part 3 – And I'm not sorry to tell you so
25. Oh Canada - Part IV
26. Enslaved

27. The Mirror
28. I don't mean to be racist, but
29. I'm not racist, I have Black Friends
30. I'm not racist, I have White Friends
31. I don't understand
32. Let me explain
33. The Mad King
34. 1 - Go back to your own country
35. 2 - No! You go back first
36. Oh Canada - Part V
37. A Legacy of Hate
38. Being Brown
39. Dr. Racist
40. Judge Racist
41. Officer Racist
42. Shades
43. Black Lives Matter
44. Jameila's Reflections
45. The Reality of our Lives
46. I don't want to World
47. Duality
48. Colour Blindness

## Janet L. Wheat-Kaytor

Janet L. Wheat-Kaytor started writing poetry as a teen. It was a medium of expression like none other. Although Wheat-Kaytor continued to write over the years, she always kept these poems to personal and apart. Brian Sankarsingh asked to see some of her poetry, and she shared some of them. This is a difficult thing to do as they represented a part of her deepest self.

After reading her poems, Sankarsingh asked her to be a contributor to this book. Wheat-Kaytor stills continues to write poetry, and hopefully one day will complete her own book.

Register of poems
ERA 3

1. A book
2. 215 children
3. Not alone
4. A White perspective

## J. E. Rehel

Photo credit: Ani Castillo

Jason is a writer, editor and, since age 4, a voracious reader of anything and everything, from sacred texts to dictionaries and everything in between. Jason is also a white, cis gender, male-leaning individual whose ancestors took part in the colonization of lands Mi'kmaq territory over 12 generations. Jason holds a degree in English literature and art history from McGill (slave-owner[4]) University, and he then edited and wrote arts journalism before engaging in work as a community health advocate and communications professional. Poetry is a longstanding love of his, across many forms and centuries. Jason seeks peace and better futures for all through his words and actions, and he was and is still humbled to be part of the Enslaved project. He hopes to continue to share and deliver on its goals of increased and deepened understandings about oppression, its causes and effects, and how to disrupt it.

---

[4] https://www.mcgill.ca/about/history/who-was-james-mcgill

# Loretta Laurie Fisher

Loretta is a passionate writer, human rights activist, and community engagement worker. She works on behalf of members of society who desperately need their voices heard. As a member of Toronto's Partnership & Accountability Circle she takes her role as a respected Elder seriously.

Loretta's reports, articles, and poetry are published in various anthologies such as "Brilliance Is the Clothing I Wear!" published by Dundurn Press. Her byline is in Spring Mag: https://springmag.ca/author/laurie-fisher.

Loretta believes we must unite as one human race and actively embrace the positive changes needed to heal ourselves and the planet.

Register of poems

ERA 3
1. Abolition – Disappeared promises
2. Jim Crow across the Eras: He Never Really Died
3. How the West was raised
4. A Strange Inconsistency
5. Plantation Capitalism - A Bitter Sugar Addiction
6. Still Tricked: Justice is M.I.A.
7. Amassing Wealth is not Common Wealth

8. Part 1 - Female Black Achievers Take on the World
9. Part 2 - Female Black Achievers Take on the World
10. Random acts of Racism
11. Documented Facts
12. Destroyed
13. Micro Aggressions
14. 1ne Race
15. …for my young brother, Tony

## Sherman K Francis

Sherman K Francis was born and raised in Trinidad and Tobago in a community that did not uplift or promote excellence. Though poor, in this community everyone found ways to create or manufacture their own happiness. One could find a rare gem like his mother, whose determination ensured her three children were educated and could choose to excel or settle for mediocrity. This Sherman understood was the key to an abundance of opportunities.

At a very early age he enjoyed performing and would often provide comedy relief for his mother and two siblings before they retired for the night. Later on he participated in the arts and thus became acutely observant of his environment. This afforded him the opportunity to mature much faster than his peers and was ahead of his years in thinking and planning. He is a very talented and thoughtful artist and portrays in his work his ability to captivate and intrigue.

He is also very religious and allows nothing to interfere in his relationship with his God. Though it may not be visible from his appearance, he is very approachable and delights in working with those who are less fortunate. He relishes an opportunity to encourage and guide a youthful mind to make constructive choices. He has developed several close relationships with the elderly and some of the women have been adopted as his mothers.

He never envisioned himself being able to travel, but has thus had the opportunity to visit several countries which has broadened his worldview. He now resides in a very remote part of the United States where he writes and practices as a Naturopathic Doctor and Natural Health Consultant.

Register of poems

ERA 3
1. Rotten House
2. Trump card
3. 1 - My Brothers, White
4. 2 - My Brothers, Black

# Index

[i] Black and White: Why capitalization matters - https://www.cjr.org/analysis/language_corner_1.php
[ii] Racist America Roots, Current Realities, and Future Reparations - https://www.routledge.com/Racist-America-Roots-Current-Realities-and-Future-Reparations/Feagin-Ducey/p/book/9781138096042
[iii] Black Pain: Slavery & The Traumatic Roots Of Modern Gynecology - https://blackdoctor.org/black-pain-slavery-the-traumatic-roots-of-modern-gynecology/
[iv] I have a Dream - https://www.americanrhetoric.com/speeches/mlkihaveadream.htm
[v] The Problem With The 'Bad Apple' Theory of Police Brutality - https://aninjusticemag.com/the-problem-with-the-bad-apple-theory-of-police-brutality-6807c23e0b46
[vi] 'A few bad apples': Phrase describing rotten police officers used to have different meaning - https://abcnews.go.com/US/bad-apples-phrase-describing-rotten-police-officers-meaning/story?id=71201096
[vii] CRUISIN' FOR A BRUISIN': Bad apples give T.O. cops a black eye - https://torontosun.com/news/local-news/cruisin-for-a-bruisin-bad-apples-give-t-o-cops-a-black-eye
[viii] The Problem With The 'Bad Apple' Theory of Police Brutality - https://aninjusticemag.com/the-problem-with-the-bad-apple-theory-of-police-brutality-6807c23e0b46
[ix] BIPOC – Black, Indigenous and People of Colour – https://www.thebipocproject.org/
[x] Slavery is Canada's Best Kept Secret - https://www.cbc.ca/radio/ideas/canada-s-slavery-secret-the-Whitewashing-of-200-years-of-enslavement-1.4726313
[xi] The Associated Press announced it will not capitalize W in White - https://www.poynter.org/reporting-editing/2020/the-associated-press-announced-it-will-not-capitalize-w-in-White/
[xii] The Pervasive Reality of Anti-Black Racism in Canada The current state, and what to do about it - https://civicaction.ca/app/uploads/2021/03/realities-of-anti-black-racism-in-canada-2020-12-12-updated.pdf
[xiii] Ontario Works - https://www.mcss.gov.on.ca/en/mcss/programs/social/ow/
[xiv] Diversity and Racism in Canada: Competing views deeply divide country along gender, generational lines - https://angusreid.org/diversity-racism-

canada/
[xv] Canada agrees to 'historic reparations' for 200,000 indigenous children - https://www.rt.com/news/545210-canada-agrees-historic-reparations-indigenous-children/
[xvi] The Pervasive Reality of Anti-Black Racism in Canada
The current state, and what to do about it - https://www.bcg.com/en-ca/publications/2020/reality-of-anti-black-racism-in-canada
[xvii] People of Colour - https://www.crrf-fcrr.ca/en/resources/glossary-a-terms-en-gb-1/item/22863-people-of-colour
[xviii] The Official website of Wilma Rudolph - https://wilmarudolph.com/
[xix] Confederate symbols prove difficult to remove in many states - https://abcnews.go.com/Politics/wireStory/confederate-symbols-prove-difficult-remove-states-76853628
[xx] Post Traumatic Slave Syndrome A Literature Review on African American Community Healing and Expressive Arts Therapy - https://digitalcommons.lesley.edu/cgi/viewcontent.cgi?article=1191&context=expressive_theses
[xxi] White Privilege: Unpacking the Invisible Knapsack by Peggy McIntosh - https://nationalseedproject.org/images/documents/Knapsack_plus_Notes-Peggy_McIntosh.pdf
[xxii] What is White Privilege Really, by Cory Collins - https://www.salisbury.edu/administration/diversity-and-inclusion/_files/anti-racism/what-is-White-privilege-really.pdf
[xxiii] Understanding Reverse Racism and its impact - https://diversity.social/reverse-racism/
[xxiv] Trump and racism: What do the data say? - https://www.brookings.edu/blog/fixgov/2019/08/14/trump-and-racism-what-do-the-data-say/
[xxv] Barack Obama – The 44th President of the United States - https://www.Whitehouse.gov/about-the-White-house/presidents/barack-obama/
[xxvi] I Have a Dream - https://www.americanrhetoric.com/speeches/mlkihaveadream.htm
[xxvii] Donald Trump, the Bible, and White Supremacy - https://hds.harvard.edu/news/2020/06/12/donald-trump-bible-and-White-supremacy
[xxviii] Racism and Health - https://www.cdc.gov/healthequity/racism-disparities/index.html
[xxix] Implicit Racial/Ethnic Bias Among Health Care Professionals and Its

Influence on Health Care Outcomes: A Systematic Review - https://www.ncbi.nlm.nih.gov/pmc/articles/PMC4638275/

[xxx] Hippocratic Oath - https://en.wikipedia.org/wiki/Hippocratic_Oath

[xxxi] Toronto-area rapper blames systemic racism for months of misdiagnosis - https://www.ctvnews.ca/health/toronto-area-rapper-blames-systemic-racism-for-months-of-misdiagnosis-1.4716013

[xxxii] How we fail black patients in pain - https://www.aamc.org/news-insights/how-we-fail-black-patients-pain

[xxxiii] Racism in the Justice System - https://www.crrf-fcrr.ca/en/site-content/item/23497-racism-in-the-justice-system

[xxxiv] Prisoners of War: The Mass Incarceration of BIPOC Communities Through the War on Drugs - https://injusticesystem.blog/2020/09/10/prisoners-of-war-the-mass-incarceration-of-bipoc-communities-through-the-war-on-drugs/

[xxxv] Judge: Female Medical Student Who Stabbed Man Is "Too Intelligent And Pretty" For Jail - https://www.returnofkings.com/122071/judge-female-medical-student-who-stabbed-man-is-too-intelligent-and-pretty-for-jail

[xxxvi] CRRF Facts about Racism and Policing - https://www.crrf-fcrr.ca/images/stories/pdf/ePubFaShRacPol.pdf

[xxxvii] History Of Racism In Policing In The United States - https://www.theodysseyonline.com/racism-police-unitedstates-history

[xxxviii] Getting Rich From the Skin Lightening Trade - https://www.businessoffashion.com/articles/beauty/profiting-from-the-skin-lightening-trade/

www.ingramcontent.com/pod-product-compliance
Lightning Source LLC
Chambersburg PA
CBHW020927090426
42736CB00010B/1060